Your Happy Healthy Pet™

Yorkshire Terrier

2nd Edition

GET MORE!
Visit www.wiley.com/
go/yorkshire_terrier

Marion Lane

Howell Book House™

Library of Congress Cataloging-in-Publication Data:
Lane, Marion.
    Yorkshire terrier/Marion Lane—2nd e.
        p.cm—(Your happy healthy pet)
    Includes index
    ISBN-10: 0-7645-8385-9 (cloth)
    ISBN-13: 978-0-7645-8385-8 (cloth)
    1. Yorkshire terrier. I. Title. II. Series.
    SF429.Y6L36   2005
    636.76—dc22
                                                   2005002073

Printed in the United States of America

10   9   8   7   6   5   4   3

2nd Edition

Book design by Melissa Auciello-Brogan
Cover design by Michael J. Freeland
Illustrations in chapter 9 by Shelley Norris and Karl Brandt
Book production by Wiley Publishing, Inc. Composition Services

About the Author

Marion Lane is a twenty-year veteran writer and editor who specializes in dogs. Her extensive knowledge of purebred dogs was acquired during the eleven years she worked for the American Kennel Club in New York City, where she was the editor of the *AKC Gazette*. To date, Lane has written dozens of articles and four books about dogs. While at the AKC, she trained her Yorkie in obedience and studied at the International School of Dog Grooming, subsequently working as a professional groomer. Until it folded in October 2004, Lane was the editor of *Animal Watch* magazine, the official publication of the American Society for the Prevention of Cruelty to Animals. For many years she has worked one day a week in her local veterinary hospital, where many, many Yorkshire Terriers are patients. Her current animal companions include two dogs, three cats, and a rabbit.

About Howell Book House

Since 1961, Howell Book House has been America's premier publisher of pet books. We're dedicated to companion animals and the people who love them, and our books reflect that commitment. Our stable of authors—training experts, veterinarians, breeders, and other authorities—is second to none. And we've won more Maxwell Awards from the Dog Writers Association of America than any other publisher.

As we head toward the half-century mark, we're more committed than ever to providing new and innovative books, along with the classics our readers have grown to love. This year, we're launching several exciting new initiatives, including redesigning the Howell Book House logo and revamping our biggest pet series, Your Happy Healthy Pet™, with bold new covers and updated content. From bringing home a new puppy to competing in advanced equestrian events, Howell has the titles that keep animal lovers coming back again and again.

Contents

Shopping List

You'll need to do a bit of stocking up before you bring your new dog or puppy home. Following is a basic list of some must-have supplies. For more detailed information on the selection of each item, consult chapter 5. For specific guidance on what grooming tools you'll need, review chapter 7.

☐ Food dish   ☐ Nail clippers

☐ Water dish   ☐ Grooming tools

☐ Dog food   ☐ Chew toys

☐ Leash   ☐ Toys

☐ Collar   ☐ ID tag

☐ Crate

There are likely to be a few other items that you're dying to pick up before bringing your dog home. Use the following blanks to note any additional items you'll be shopping for.

☐ _____

☐ _____

☐ _____

☐ _____

☐ _____

☐ _____

☐ _____

☐ _____

☐ _____

☐ _____

☐ _____

☐ _____

Pet Sitter's Guide

We can be reached at (__)_____-_____ Cellphone (__)_____-_____

We will return on _____ (date) at _____ (approximate time)

Dog's Name _____

Breed, Age, and Sex _____

Important Names and Numbers

Vet's Name _____ Phone (__)_____-_____

Address_____

Emergency Vet's Name _____ Phone (__)_____-_____

Address_____

Poison Control _____ (or call vet first)

Other individual to contact in case of emergency _____

Care Instructions

In the first three blanks let the sitter know what to feed, how much, and when; when the dog should go out; when to give treats; and when to exercise the dog.

Morning _____

_____

Afternoon _____

_____

Evening _____

_____

Medications needed (dosage and schedule) _____

_____

Any special medical conditions _____

_____

Grooming instructions _____

_____

My dog's favorite playtime activities, quirks, and other tips _____

_____

_____

Part I

The World of the
Yorkshire Terrier

The Yorkshire Terrier

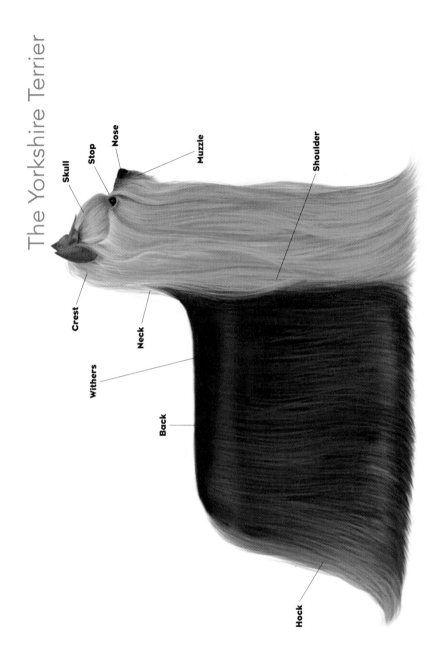

Nose

Stop

Muzzle

Skull

Shoulder

Crest

Neck

Withers

Back

Hock

Chapter 1

What Is a Yorkshire Terrier?

T he first time I thought about Yorkshire Terriers was in 1978 when my boyfriend, Bill, decided a Yorkie was what he wanted to give me for my birthday. Fortunately, Bill knew that no one should surprise anyone with a dog, and he wisely wanted me to pick out my own puppy. In my heart, of course, I knew that Bill wanted this puppy as much for himself as for me, but I didn't mind. I happily threw myself into the project of researching the Yorkshire Terrier.

The first thing I did was buy two Yorkshire Terrier breed books. The first was more of an illustrated booklet, and I honestly don't know if I did much more than drool over the pictures. It was only later, when I saw my first Yorkie in the flesh, that I realized the glamorous pictures had given me a false impression of this energetic little dog.

The second book was a substantial but slow-going study of the breed, more suited to Yorkie historians, breeders, and serious fanciers than to first-time pet owners. Only after I'd lived with a Yorkie for several years did I go back and take another look at those two books. Neither one had prepared me for either the challenges or the special joys of living with this breed. That's why every word of this book was written with that memory in mind.

The Yorkie Standard

Yorkie! The very name suggests something tiny, cute, and perky, and the Yorkshire Terrier is certainly all of these things. As a well-established purebred

What Is a Breed Standard?

A breed standard is a detailed description of the perfect dog of that breed. Breeders use the standard as a guide in their breeding programs, and judges use it to evaluate the dogs in conformation shows. The standard is written by the national breed club, using guidelines established by the registry that recognizes the breed (such as the AKC or UKC).

The first section of the breed standard gives a brief overview of the breed's history. Then it describes the dog's general appearance and size as an adult. Next is a detailed description of the head and neck, then the back and body, and the front and rear legs. The standard then describes the ideal coat and how the dog should be presented in the show ring. It also lists all acceptable colors, patterns, and markings. Then there's a section on how the dog moves, called *gait*. Finally, there's a general description of the dog's temperament.

Each section also lists characteristics that are considered to be faults or disqualifications in the conformation ring. Superficial faults in appearance are often what distinguish a pet-quality dog from a show or competition-quality dog. However, some faults affect the way a dog moves or his overall health. And faults in temperament are serious business.

You can read all the AKC breed standards at www.akc.org.

dog, the Yorkie's unique physical aspects (known collectively as "type"), as well as his character traits, are spelled out in a document called the breed standard.

If you're anything like I was when I got my Yorkie, you probably think show dogs and dog shows are weird, and you don't have a clue what this standard has to do with the dog you're about to get for a companion. As it turns out, quite a lot!

The official Yorkshire Terrier standard is a kind of blueprint for breeders and judges. The standard ensures that none of the historically important features that characterize the Yorkie will be lost in future generations. A puppy doesn't have to meet the standard in every way to make a suitable pet. On the other

The Yorkshire Terrier is a regal, solid little dog.

hand, since the standard spells out all those things that make a Yorkie different from any other dog, it stands to reason that you'd want a puppy whose breeder had that in mind when they set out to create the magical creature who's coming to live at your house.

So how does the standard describe a Yorkshire Terrier? If the human eye is pleased by balance and symmetry, the Yorkie is a sight for sore eyes indeed. The small head is in proportion with the compact body; the little prick ears on one end complement the docked tail on the other. With the whole package draped in steel-blue silk, the Yorkie looks like he belongs on the knee of a monarch.

Looks can be deceiving, though, and the term "toy" should not be taken literally. The Yorkie is a for-real dog. If you treat your Duke of York like a toy, you may end up with a spoiled, even snappy, seven-pound tyrant (sometimes called the "Yorkshire Terrorist"). You will also deprive yourself of the joy of experiencing firsthand the Duke's legendary charm and cheek.

The Yorkie's tough spirit balances his small size.

In other words, while the Yorkie's coat, size, and color surely are his most unique physical characteristics, it's the terrier in the Yorkie that gives him his "hey you!" attitude. Those of us who love Yorkies love the complete package: tiny size, glossy good looks, keen intelligence, and big-dog outlook on life.

The standard states that the Yorkie is compact and well proportioned. Underneath his very long coat, his crowning glory, the Yorkie's body is athletic and sturdy, designed for a long, active life. Important physical features are his short, level back (hips and shoulders are the same height) and his straight legs with moderately bent stifles (knees). The Yorkie also has a moderately long neck (important for carrying the head high) and enough forechest (the part that sticks out in front of the legs when viewed from the side) to house a good set of lungs for stamina. When trotting along on a loose leash, the Yorkie has a free, jaunty gait, with both head and tail held high. In the Yorkie, small does not mean frail or fragile.

It's important for all Yorkies, whether show dogs or simply companions, to have these basic physical features. Along with health and conditioning, it's a dog's underlying structure that determines the kinds of activities, or lifestyle, he can engage in. In the Yorkie's case, this includes, at the very least, long walks (preferably where there are squirrels to chase), brisk games of catch in the backyard or the park, and spirited sessions of tug in the living room. Many people think rigorous activities are dangerous for small dogs. This is nonsense. A well-built Yorkie is able to do just about anything that a larger dog can do—just on a shorter scale.

In perfect balance with the Yorkie's rugged little frame is his tough little spirit. The confident manner mentioned in the standard is as much a part of the Yorkshire Terrier as are his size and coat. The Yorkie's bearing must clearly convey that this is a vigorous small dog of considerable importance. But when you're ankle high on the leg of the average human, how do you get that message across? With a look. And the physical features that do the most to make up the typical look of the Yorkie are his eyes and ears.

Yorkie eyes are dark, and they sparkle with intelligence. His small, erect, mobile ears are like radar dishes that telegraph the Yorkie's lively interest in everything around him. Although the ears are tipped over in very young puppies, they should stand erect by the time the dog is about 3 months old; a Yorkie without fully erect ears will never have the typical Yorkie expression. Overall, the expression of the breed is alert, inquisitive, and self-confident.

The Yorkie breed standard is very particular when it comes to coat color. It says, "Puppies are born black and tan and are normally darker in body color, showing an intermingling of black hair in the tan until they are matured. Color of hair on body and richness of tan on head and legs are of prime importance in adult dogs, to which the following color requirements apply:

"BLUE: Is a dark steel-blue, not a silver-blue and not mingled with fawn, bronzy or black hairs.

What Is a Breed Club?

A breed club is an association of dog breeders, fanciers, and ordinary pet owners who gather together for the purpose of promoting the interests of a specific breed. In accordance with the requirements of the American Kennel Club (AKC), breed clubs must offer speciality (one-breed) dog shows every year, sanctioned matches (informal dog shows), and educational events that are intended to educate the general public about purebred dogs in general and their breed in particular.

Breed clubs are either national or local. A national club has no address. Its officers come from across the country, and its primary activity is to stage one national specialty show a year. If a national club is a member of the AKC, it is called the parent club for the breed. Among a parent club's most important obligations is maintaining the breed standard. No changes can be made to the official breed standard except through the parent club. Changes are rarely made; the Yorkshire Terrier breed standard was last amended in 1966.

For information on the Yorkshire Terrier Club of America and local Yorkshire Terrier clubs, see the appendix.

"TAN: All tan hair is darker at the roots than in the middle, shading to still lighter tan at the tips. There should be no sooty or black hair intermingled with any of the tan."

Coat texture is also described in some detail. The standard says, "Quality, texture and quantity of coat are of prime importance. Hair is glossy, fine and silky in texture. Coat on the body is moderately long and perfectly straight (not wavy). It may be trimmed to floor length to give ease of movement and a neater appearance, if desired. . . ."

When I first read this, I had not yet seen a real, live Yorkie. I wondered how anyone could get so worked up over a few dark hairs mixed in with the tan ones, or care so much whether the blue looked like steel rather than silver. It all seemed rather extreme. Clearly a Yorkie whose coat color, length, or texture was not quite up to the standard was no less desirable as a pet!

The Yorkie's beautiful look and lively spirit are timeless.

Then a long-time Yorkie fancier pointed out that the standard has changed very little since it was written in 1912. He asked me this: "How many car models, hair styles, hem lengths, dance steps, and music crazes have come and gone in the same eighty-odd years?" The point is that if breeders didn't hold to an exacting standard with regard to coat, it wouldn't be long before the Yorkie lost his distinctive look. And isn't that what drew me (and you) to Yorkies in the first place?

Companion or Show Quality?

I bought my Yorkie from an Englishwoman named Joan who worked for the United Nations. The puppy was one of a litter of two females. I chose the puppy who was most daring and outgoing. Joan had named her Mary, but I had already decided to call her Lilli. Then Bill began to call her The Wee, and that stuck.

In my pride and prejudice, I thought The Wee would turn out to be a show dog. It was clear she was not bred from show lines, and my Yorkie breed book (the serious one) stated flatly that no silk purses will come from sow's ears where Yorkshire Terriers are concerned. Still, by the time she was 6 months old, the change in The Wee's appearance was so dramatic that I just knew she was going to be the exception to the rule.

A pet-quality dog may not have the same long, flowing coat as a show dog, but he should have the same take-charge attitude.

Then, in February 1979, I went to the Westminster Kennel Club dog show at Madison Square Garden in New York. It took only one good look to see that there was no way The Wee was ever going to grow the color, texture, or amount of coat that show Yorkies have. In time I was able to see that she had just as many faults in other areas. Nonetheless, she was unmistakably a Yorkie and unmistakably a toy terrier. In terms of confidence, vigor, and self-importance, she not only met but exceeded the breed standard.

In simplest terms, the difference between show-quality and companion-quality Yorkies is the extent to which they meet the standard. Still, the range of companion- or pet-quality Yorkies is extremely broad. It covers everything from a well-bred puppy with just a few too many dark hairs intermingled with the tan to the sentimental litter out of Aunt Sally's Freddy and her next-door neighbor's Maxine. But since it is the official standard that describes the ideal Yorkshire Terrier, and it is only *because* of the standard that the Yorkshire Terrier type has survived to this day, I believe that breeding Yorkies should be left to those who follow the standard. That means only a small percentage of the roughly 38,000 Yorkies registered by the AKC each year are suitable to be show (and breeding) stock. But, happily, every single one of them is suitable to be the world's best companion to you or me!

Chapter 2

The Yorkshire Terrier's Ancestry

If the only Yorkshire Terriers you ever saw were show dogs in full coat and bow-tied topknots, you'd have a hard time imagining how on earth—and why—such a creature had come into existence. There's no question that today's Yorkie is first and foremost a companion dog. Although all dogs are willing and able to be someone's true-blue pal, few breeds were deliberately developed for that reason. If you go far enough back in the history of any pure breed of dog, you're bound to discover an original utilitarian purpose. The Yorkshire Terrier is no exception.

The Origin of Breeds

In nature, dogs do not vary widely. In different parts of the world, a few basic types evolved from the wolf, in keeping with local climate and terrain. Virtually all of the exaggerated physical characteristics—such as very large or very small size, great coat length or density, and structural extremes such as large heads, flat faces, pendulous ears, and elongated bodies—were selected for by humans to enhance the dog's usefulness in some way.

Likewise, when locally available dogs showed special ability or enthusiasm for specific tasks, people naturally bred these animals to try to "fix" (permanently establish) these attributes and pass them on to future generations of puppies. And this is exactly what led to the unique group that includes the Yorkie's forebears.

The Terrier Factor

The group of dogs called terriers was developed in the fourteenth through nineteenth centuries, mostly in the British Isles. Throughout most of its early history, Britain had been a two-class society. The upper classes owned the land and all that grew, lived, or moved upon it, and the lower peasant class owned the shirts on their backs, if they were lucky.

At that time, an important source of meat for lordly tables was the furred, feathered, and tusked wild game of the forests and fields. To help bring down this game, noblemen employed huntsmen, who in turn used large coursing hounds. The peasants, however, were prohibited from taking game from the royal forests. The penalty for "stealing" the king's deer, for instance, was hanging. To help enforce the law, peasants were also prohibited from owning any of the large breeds of dogs suitable for hunting. Small dogs, however, were permitted, and there wasn't likely to be much objection if the dogs hunted the small, unsavory varmints that lived belowground. Thus, the stage was set for a historical association between the poor and a small, rugged dog with a strong hunting instinct.

To understand your Yorkie, you have to understand terriers. What distinguishes the terriers from other kinds of dogs is their strong drive to dig. The word "terrier" is derived from the French term *chien terrier,* meaning "dog of the earth." As a hunting group, terriers specialize in pursuing animals (usually vermin rather than game) who live in dens or burrows. Animals who are cornered in their dens, and/or are defending their young, will fight ferociously. Therefore, any dog who would willingly pursue them had to have an uncommon degree of courage. The kind of dog that most admirably filled the twin bills of small size and large heart was the terrier.

In the field, terriers have been used to drive quarry from its burrow for pursuit by hounds, to hold quarry at bay until hunters with guns could arrive, or to dig quarry out and engage it themselves. In many cases, terriers were encouraged to hunt independently, living and dying by their own decisions.

Terriers further developed as specialists in different terrain and for

Famous Yorkshire Terrier Owners

Cindy Adams

Helen Hayes

Audrey Hepburn

Tama Janowitz

Liberace

Barbara Mandrell

Richard Nixon

Gilda Radner

Joan Rivers

Amy Tan

Justin Timberlake

different quarry species. In general, the English terriers were longer legged, with smooth coats and folded ears, and hunted fox, otter, woodchuck, and badger. In contrast, the Scottish terriers were short legged, with erect ears and long, harsh coats. They hunted rats, ferrets, and weasels, as well as rabbits and ground squirrels. It is from the Scottish stock that the Yorkie is descended.

The Yorkshire Terrier is part of the terrier family— breeds developed to tenaciously pursue animals who live in dens and burrows.

Anyone obtaining a terrier needs to know that the wonderful, feisty temperament they admire comes with its other, less-attractive corollary: independence. To this day, terriers as a group are considered hardheaded and difficult to train.

Made in England

As its name implies, the Yorkshire Terrier is a product of Yorkshire County in northern England. This remote and rugged region was made familiar to millions of people through the best-selling *All Creatures Great and Small* series of books, and subsequent long-running television series, by country veterinarian James Herriot. By the middle of the nineteenth century, the engine of England's industrial revolution was running full tilt in Yorkshire. In addition to agriculture and livestock production, the area's rich deposits of coal and iron helped fuel the industrial revolution's new industries, including textiles.

In search of work, weavers and other craftsmen had come to Yorkshire from Scotland, bringing with them several different varieties of small, long-coated terriers. These so-called Scottish terriers found ready work themselves in controlling the rodent populations in Yorkshire's mills, mines, and factories. On weekends, the dogs' owners were not above a bit of sport, wagering on whose terrier could dispatch the largest number of rats in a given length of time.

While experts do not agree on exactly which breeds have made up the Yorkshire Terrier, certain breeds are commonly thought to be her main forebears. The possible source of the dog's size, coat length, and blue-black color are the Clydesdale, Paisley, Skye, and Waterside Terriers—all Scottish breeds brought to England at various times. Additionally, the English Black and Tan

This is the only known painting made during the lifetime of Huddersfield Ben, the father of the breed.

Terrier seems to be the most likely candidate to have lent the Yorkie breed her signature color pattern.

One bit of Yorkie history we do know for sure is that in 1865, in or around the town of Huddersfield in Yorkshire County, a dog named Ben was born. In his short life (he died of an accident when he was only 6 years old), he won many prizes at dog shows and also in ratting contests. By today's standards, Ben was a large dog with only a medium-length coat, no doubt partly due to the active life he led. This dog, known as Huddersfield Ben, is universally acknowledged as the father of the Yorkshire Terrier.

The Yorkie in America

The Yorkie has been a popular breed in the United States since the turn of the twentieth century. Yorkies have been entered in dog shows in America since 1878. The first Yorkie was registered with the American Kennel Club in 1885, making it one of the first twenty-five breeds to be approved for registration by the AKC. Yorkies have been in high demand ever since as one of the most popular toy breeds.

In 1978, a Yorkie won the coveted Best in Show at the prestigious Westminster Kennel Club show—the first and only member of the breed ever to do so. The dog to win this prize was Ch. Cede Higgens, a male owned by Charles and Barbara Switzer of Seattle, Washington.

Yorkies, You, and Me

American Yorkies are predominantly house and apartment dogs, often living in multiple-Yorkie households, supporting the idea that if one is good, more are better, and many are best! For obvious reasons, Yorkies have great appeal for people with limited space, and because they are small enough to be paper- or litter box–trained, they are ideal companions for busy people who may get stuck at the office.

Still, it's important to remember that your Yorkie is very much a dog and therefore will love to be out and about in the world. Some people argue that if Yorkies are never taken out, they won't miss it. But I feel strongly that a Yorkie simply can never be all that nature intended her to be unless she gets the chance to snuffle in a fragrant patch of earth and feel the power her own ferocious barking has upon an errant flock of pigeons in the park. As Yorkie owners, we need to be very honest about whose best interests we have in mind if we deprive our wee terriers of their instinctive joys.

Any Yorkshire Terrier can be active in all kinds of canine competitions.

What Is the AKC?

The American Kennel Club (AKC) is the oldest and largest pure-bred dog registry in the United States. Its main function is to record the pedigrees of dogs of the breeds it recognizes. While AKC registration papers are a guarantee that a dog is pure-bred, they are absolutely not a guarantee of the quality of the dog—as the AKC itself will tell you.

The AKC makes the rules for all the canine sporting events it sanctions and approves judges for those events. It is also involved in various public education programs and legislative efforts regarding dog ownership. More recently, the AKC has helped establish a foundation to study canine health issues and a program to register microchip numbers for companion animal owners. The AKC has no individual members—its members are national and local breed clubs and clubs dedicated to various competitive sports.

As previously stated, only Yorkies who are specifically bred, conditioned, and trained for the show ring will have any chance of competing there. For those who are interested, there are many other kinds of competitive activities where ability, not appearance, is what counts. For example, any registered Yorkie, including spayed or neutered ones, can compete in AKC-licensed obedience, tracking, and agility trials, which, while beyond the scope of this book, can be investigated through the resources listed in the appendix. A Yorkie need not even be registered to participate in programs such as the Canine Good Citizen or pet therapy.

More important than any organized activity are all the everyday kinds of things that you can do with your wee one. These activities don't require going to a class or being tested or certified. Just remember, anything you and your Yorkie do together will make her a better companion, you a better dog owner, and your relationship deeper and more gratifying than you ever thought possible.

Chapter 3

Why Choose a Yorkshire Terrier?

I f you've drooled over the dainty Yorkies at dog shows who lie on satin pillows and look like they wouldn't say "boo" to a mouse, do not expect your Eliza Doolittle dog to look or act like that. At heart, the Yorkie is still a scrappy working-class terrier who has had no say in the matter of becoming a lap dog. The typical Yorkie personality easily fills the frame of a dog many times his size. If there's one wrong way to go about living with a Yorkie, it is to treat this tiny toy dog like a tiny toy!

What Makes a Yorkie Tick?

There's no denying that Yorkies are captivating little imps, filled with energy, high spirits, and an inexhaustible enthusiasm for life. Yorkies are also smart and easily trained. If yours doesn't seem to be any of those things, you may be working against, rather than with, the Yorkie's basic nature and temperament. The Wee and I did not get off to a very good start, partly because I was intimidated by her tiny size but mostly because I just didn't appreciate how much terrier is still in the Yorkshire.

Lest you get the idea that Yorkies are God's perfect creatures, let me hasten to tell you that a Yorkie has the same capacity as the next dog to become spoiled, uncooperative, disagreeable, and even aggressive. Obviously a dog so small—and Yorkie puppies are *very* small—needs to be protected from potential hazards and handled gently (more about this in later chapters). But aside from some health and safety considerations, you'll be far ahead of the game if you pretend

The Dog's Senses

The dog's eyes are designed so that he can see well in relative darkness, has excellent peripheral vision, and is very good at tracking moving objects—all skills that are important to a carnivore. Dogs also have good depth perception. Those advantages come at a price, though: Dogs are nearsighted and are slow to change the focus of their vision. It's a myth that dogs are colorblind. However, while they can see some (but not all) colors, their eyes were designed to most clearly perceive subtle shades of gray—an advantage when they are hunting in low light.

Dogs have about six times fewer taste buds on their tongue than humans do. They can taste sweet, sour, bitter, and salty tastes, but with so few taste buds it's likely that their sense of taste is not very refined.

A dog's ears can swivel independently, like radar dishes, to pick up sounds and pinpoint their location. Dogs can locate a sound in $\frac{6}{100}$ of a second and hear sound four times farther away than we can (which is why there is no reason to yell at your dog). They can also hear sounds at far higher pitches than we can.

In their first few days of life, puppies primarily use their sense of touch to navigate their world. Whiskers on the face, above the eyes, and below the jaws are sensitive enough to detect changes in airflow. Dogs also have touch-sensitive nerve endings all over their bodies, including on their paws.

Smell may be a dog's most remarkable sense. Dogs have about 220 million scent receptors in their nose, compared to about 5 million in humans, and a large part of the canine brain is devoted to interpreting scent. Not only can dogs smell scents that are very faint, but they can also accurately distinguish between those scents. In other words, when you smell a pot of spaghetti sauce cooking, your dog probably smells tomatoes and onions and garlic and oregano and whatever else is in the pot.

that your puppy will grow up to weigh forty pounds. Then every time you're tempted to treat him like an orchid, you'll stop yourself.

Yorkie Character

Like all dogs, Yorkies have the full range of canine behaviors. They're social creatures who like to know where they fit into the household pack. They quickly sort out who belongs and who doesn't, they will bark at strangers, they'll be friendly and outgoing or unfriendly and aloof (largely based on how you train them to be), and, of course, they chew and dig and scratch and groom themselves in front of company. Yorkie owners sometimes forget that their pets speak dog, not English, which means you have to learn how to communicate with them, not the other way around.

It's also important to realize that every dog is an individual. Some parts of a dog's temperament are inherited from his parents, and while it's not typical (that is, not what the standard calls for), a few individual Yorkies may be timid or nervous rather than bold. Puppies whose first weeks aren't spent in a loving home with a conscientious breeder may get a bad start in life that will show up as atypical temperament and behavior; these characteristics can sometimes be overcome, but sometimes they can't. Fortunately, the vast majority of Yorkies do seem to be just what the standard calls for: confident, vigorous, and self-important. The following are some of the qualities that are likely to show up in your dog.

The vast majority of Yorkies are confident and self-important.

A Yorkshire Terrier is tenacious and smart—qualities that may get him into trouble.

Tenacity

Yorkies have astonishing drive and stick-to-it-ness, which are, of course, hunting attributes. Why, then, do we often hear that they're willful and stubborn? In truth, tenacity and willfulness are really the same qualities—the only difference is whether the task at hand is performed with your encouragement or to your dismay. Take a Yorkie into the ordinary, repetitive obedience training class, for example, and you'll see willfulness as art form. Give your Yorkie something intrinsically interesting to do, such as chase down and retrieve a floppy object that lends itself to a good shaking and you'll lose count of the number of times he'll want you to play this game with him.

Tenacity is most likely to show up when the Yorkie is in his hunting mode. Never mind that the quarry is a knotted sock or a favorite ball that has rolled out of reach under a table. The Yorkie may well take up a daylong vigil, ignoring repeated calls to dinner and other favorite activities. Even a bit of dog biscuit can set the Yorkie off on a three-hour search for the perfect place to bury it among the sofa pillows.

Boldness

Many Yorkie owners tell proud but harrowing tales of the day their mini Cujo took on the rogue Rottweiler down the street, and it's a rare multibreed home with a Yorkshire Terrier where the top dog is not the Yorkie. Note, however, that bold does not mean aggressive. Bold is what you get when you mix great inquisitiveness, or the instinct to protect, with self-confidence.

Some time ago, a television program about dogs featured a segment in which a single woman's Yorkie sent the woman's date to the emergency room for stitches when the dog misconstrued the gentleman's friendly smack on the lady's rump. The funny part was that the suffering suitor claimed his assailant was a German Shepherd; apparently admitting to being attacked by a five-pound Yorkshire Terrier would have added insult to injury.

Whether or not you're amused by your Yorkie's boldness, never lose sight of the fact that he can get himself into trouble. No matter how large his ego, he is still a little dog and can be seriously injured.

Intelligence

Yorkies are smart dogs. They do well in sports such as obedience and agility that require the dog to carry out a complex series of commands and where success depends on the ability of the dog and the handler to communicate with each other. Pet Yorkies learn to recognize an astonishing number of words, distinguish and fetch separate toys from a box by their names, and are generally very rewarding for the teacher who likes an apt pupil.

Yorkies also have an uncanny ability to make complex chains of associations—when there's something in it for them. For example, if you get in the habit of taking your Sampson for a ride in the car on Sunday mornings to pick up the newspaper at the shop across town, where once in awhile the shopkeeper gives him a bit of liverwurst, it will not be long before Sam heads for the front door at the first pealing of a distant church bell. The Wee so loved her walks that we learned never to say the word in vain, and even resorted to spelling it—a solution that worked for a little while before she decoded that, too.

High Activity Level

Most tiny dogs are active and quick, and the Yorkie is no exception. Someone used to a St. Bernard would be apt to label a Yorkie as hyperactive. In describing the behavior of the normally active Yorkie, words like "darting," "dashing," "scampering," "hopping," and "bouncing" come to mind. A Yorkie who actually *walks* on his daily walks is quite likely ancient, ill, or possibly too hot.

Be aware that Yorkies do have a lot to say. It's the terrier in them that prompts the need to bark . . . and bark . . . and bark. On the other hand, when the Yorkie barks, there's always a reason. Yorkies make excellent watchdogs. They sleep lightly, awaken in a heartbeat, and are in motion (and in voice) in the time it takes a larger, more placid dog to lift his head from the floor.

Independence

This final Yorkie characteristic may seem inconsistent with the others, but the well-bred, and especially the well-handled, Yorkie can be quite content to be near you without necessarily being under your feet at every moment. Yorkies throw themselves into whatever they do, but their small bodies have small fuel tanks, and left to their own resources, they know when they need to rest. At

Your tough, independent dog may be inclined to make choices that are not good for him. It's your job to protect him without coddling him.

these times, the Yorkie is likely to disappear behind the shoes in your closet or into a warm, out-of-the-way corner for some down time.

A forerunner to this trait can be found in the Yorkie's ancestry: Terriers were expected to hunt in the company of handlers or other dogs but also to have the self-confidence to go out on their own after prey. Owners who are not prepared for their Yorkshire Terrier's independence may feel hurt and disappointed when confronted with this trait. On the other hand, pampered and indulged Yorkies are more likely to be clingy and demanding, while ironically lacking in true terrier self-confidence.

Chapter 4

Choosing Your Yorkshire Terrier

Okay! You have a good idea of what to expect in a Yorkie, and you can't wait. It's time to take the next step—finding a puppy. This could be the most important decision you'll make in your dog-owning journey, so listen up: Don't be in such a hurry that you lay down your money—and your heart—for the first Yorkie puppy who comes along.

Where to Get Puppies

Where will you get your Yorkie? The sources of dogs—and there are basically six—are not all created equal. It's important to understand the differences among them.

Pet Shops

Pet shops supply mostly purebred puppies that are roughly 2 to 4 months old. Invariably, the puppies you will find in pet shops are the most popular breeds—which, unfortunately, includes the Yorkshire Terrier. Salespeople in pet shops may have little in-depth knowledge about dogs in general, and they are unlikely to know anything at all about the particular puppies they are offering for sale. Their primary objective is to sell their "merchandise" while it's still young and appealing, not to find the best home for that puppy in the window. As business-people, pet shop owners may want you to be a satisfied customer, but they really are not equipped to ensure that you are.

Puppies in pet shops are supplied by puppy mills, which are commercial breeding businesses that raise dogs the way farmers raise livestock: as a cash crop. Not only are many commercial breeding operations shockingly inhumane in the way the dogs are housed, fed, and maintained, but the adult dogs, and therefore the puppies, are often afflicted with health problems. This is because puppy mill operators possess neither the knowledge nor the incentive to breed and raise healthy, let alone correct (according to the breed standard), puppies. And because the puppies are taken from their mothers and littermates at a very young age and shipped to market, the puppies often have emotional and/or behavioral problems as well.

To add insult to injury, these poor-quality pet shop puppies are often more expensive than puppies from any other source. Come what may, the overhead of the shop in the mall has to be met. Registration papers may or may not be available at the time of purchase (which they should be), and more and more often these days, the pups may be registered with an unknown organization rather than with the AKC. Unsuspecting puppy purchasers may be misled by this.

Backyard Breeders

These casual breeders include our friends, relatives, and neighbors and account for most of the puppies advertised in local newspapers. Whether they are motivated by the hope of making money or just by the desire to have a puppy from their beloved pet, these "breeders" typically know very little about canine health, genetics, temperament, and behavior. They probably bought the dog they are breeding from a pet store and will inevitably breed her to another dog with the same unknown background. Once the litter is born, they're likely to be more interested in finding buyers for their puppies than in making sure you and your puppy are a wonderful match.

Puppies may or may not have received early veterinary care, socialization, or basic handling and housetraining. Yorkies' tails should be docked before the pups are a week old, but many backyard breeders are unaware of this or don't want to spend the money. Backyard-bred puppies generally cost much less than pet store puppies, and "papers" (that is, AKC registration papers) are often unavailable.

Responsible Breeders

Responsible breeders—also called hobby or professional breeders—are very knowledgeable about Yorkshire Terriers and the strengths and weaknesses of their own dogs. They are members of the Yorkshire Terrier Club of America, which means they subscribe to the club's code of ethics regarding breeding dogs and selling puppies. They breed litters only occasionally and may offer puppies of different ages as well as occasional adolescent and adult dogs.

Responsible hobby breeders, in general, are very thorough in screening potential buyers—you should be prepared to have to prove yourself and your home "suitable" to own one of their puppies—but once they've found you worthy, they offer a great deal of follow-up support on diet, training, and living with your dog.

If you buy a puppy from a responsible breeder, you can expect to be offered a contract that will provide some protection to both you and the breeder. Many hobby breeders will take back (even insist on having returned) a puppy who doesn't work out for any reason, at any time. Mother dogs will have received good prenatal care, and puppies from this source often have had substantial early socialization and training in the breeder's home—all of which will make your job so much easier. Puppies from hobby breeders are not cheap but generally cost less than pet store puppies.

Responsible breeders start your puppy off right with gentle handling and socialization.

Animal Shelters

Twenty-five percent of the dogs in animal shelters across the United States are purebred, and no animal is more deserving of a great home than a dog who has ended up in a shelter, by whatever route. Despite public perceptions, most dogs are *not* there because there is something wrong with them.

Modern shelters do a very good job of matchmaking a pet with a new home, but supply and demand being what they are, you'd have to be very lucky to find a Yorkshire Terrier of any age available at your local shelter. By all means make a visit and get on a waiting list, but don't hold your breath waiting for the telephone to ring. Yorkies are too much in demand to find their way to shelters very often. Those who are found on the street will most likely be kept by their rescuers or given to a friend or family member.

Breed Rescue

Breed rescue groups are, in essence, private single-breed networks of hobby breeders and fanciers who offer foster homes to homeless dogs and occasionally puppies of that breed until they are ready for adoption. All of the AKC national breed clubs have a breed rescue committee that is charged with coordinating rescue efforts across the country. Yorkies find their way to rescue in a number of ways. Some are found dogs, and some are rescued from failed commercial breeding operations.

Dogs adopted from breed rescue groups usually have been screened for health and temperament, rehabilitated if necessary, then kept in foster care until permanent homes can be found. Rescue dogs are not sold, but adopters usually are required to reimburse the group for veterinary and other costs that have been incurred. Follow-up assistance to deal with any problems is usually provided, and adopters are required to return their dog to the rescue group if she cannot be kept for any reason.

Found Dogs

Found dogs are complete unknowns. There are as many reasons they are at large as there are at-large dogs. Whether they find you or you find them, there's often

Puppies and adults both make great pets.

a sense of destiny about the meeting that overrides practical considerations regarding suitability, timing, convenience, and any preconceived ideas about what kind of dog you're looking for—or even if you're looking for a dog at all. Giving a home to a Yorkie you find wandering down the street is very much a matter of making the best of it, and many of these acquisitions don't work out well for dog or owner, although large numbers certainly do.

Because taking in a stray dog is usually an impulsive if noble act, it cannot be recommended as a way to find a companion for the long run. In addition, it must be noted that the dog you find is not, morally or legally, yours to keep. That Yorkie may have an owner who is desperately looking for their pet, and your obligation is to take

> ## Is an Adult Yorkie Right for You?
>
> When most of us start thinking about getting a dog, we automatically set our sights on a puppy. But as irresistable as they are, puppies are a lot of work. It will be difficult for busy working people to give a demanding baby the good start she deserves.
>
> Fortunately, there are alternatives to the 8- or 10-week-old puppy, who has housetraining, teething (read chewing), spaying or neutering, a growing coat, and puppy classes to get through in her first six months with you. Teenaged, young adult, and even mature dogs often are looking for homes, and one of these deserving nonpups may be the perfect solution to balancing your desire for a Yorkie with a limited amount of time to devote to raising a puppy. A hobby breeder or breed rescue group is your best source for adult Yorkies.

that dog to your local shelter where dog and owner have the best chance of being reunited. If no owner comes forward and you're interested in adopting the dog, you can always ask to be notified, and most shelter staff will be happy to do so.

Finding a Responsible Breeder

I hope I have convinced you that your best bet for a healthy, happy puppy is a responsible breeder. Now, how do you go about finding one? Unfortunately, they aren't listed under R in the telephone directory. And because selling puppies is not a "business" to responsible breeders, they can be a little hard to find. Here are some ways to locate that all-important person.

Ask Around

When you see what looks like a nice, small, typical Yorkie who's well-groomed and appears to be bright and outgoing, ask the owner where they got their dog. If the answer is "a private breeder," ask more questions about the dog's health and temperament and how satisfied the owner is with their pet and with their

Dog shows are an excellent place to meet Yorkie breeders and learn about the breed.

relationship with the breeder. If the answers are positive, ask for the breeder's contact information.

Local veterinarians can also be a good resource to find owners (and sometimes breeders) of nice, healthy Yorkies, but be aware that they won't likely give you contact information for their clients without getting permission first.

Go to Dog Shows

Thousands of dog shows are held around the country all year long, and these are ideal places to see Yorkies and to meet breeders and exhibitors of quality dogs. All-breed shows almost always have Yorkies entered, and Yorkie specialty shows, although far less common, will have nothing but Yorkshire Terriers. Dog shows are usually advertised in local newspapers, but you can also find out when and where shows are held by contacting the AKC, either by telephone or online. (See the appendix for contact information.)

Search Online

The Internet is *the* modern way to find anything and everything. But beware: Anyone can claim to be a responsible breeder of Yorkshire Terriers. Visit Web sites and contact breeders (see the appendix), but keep in mind the hallmarks of responsible breeders I discussed earlier in this chapter.

A responsible breeder will be a member of the Yorkshire Terrier Club of America and possibly of a local dog club and a Yorkshire regional club, ideally, for many years. They will be breeding to the Yorkshire Terrier breed standard. They will not likely be involved in more than one other breed in addition to Yorkies, and probably not even that. They will show their Yorkies in AKC-sanctioned shows and have many champions in their line. They probably will not have any puppies available when you call and will expect you to be willing to wait until a puppy is available. You will be expected to sign a contract when you buy a puppy, and very possibly the puppy you buy will be offered on a limited registration only—meaning if you decide to breed your dog, her puppies can not be registered with the AKC. Rejoice if these conditions are imposed because it means the individual you are dealing with has the best interests of Yorkshire Terriers at heart.

Picking a Puppy

Once you've found a responsible breeder and a litter has been born, expect to have butterflies in your stomach when you go to the breeder's home to look at puppies. Chances are you've waited six months or more for the puppies to be

Picking just one can be tough!

Health Checklist

Reputable breeders will not knowingly offer sick puppies for sale, but you should still be alert and observant. The following checklist will help you detect possible problems in any puppy you're considering:

- Does the puppy appear healthy? Is she active, playful, and interested in her surroundings? A very quiet, still puppy may be ill or in pain.
- Does the puppy move naturally? Limping or favoring a limb signals pain. Also look for hesitation to move or jump and an unnatural gait, such as giving a little hop every few steps.
- Are there signs of infection? These include thick, colored, or crusty discharge from the eyes or nose; sneezing or coughing; and red, hot, inflamed ears. Dark, crumbling debris inside the ear probably means ear mites.
- Are the skin and coat clear and clean? Check for flakes and scales, sores and rashes, bare patches, offensive odor, and very dry and dull or very oily hair.

born, and you feel you've been "expecting" a long, long time (doesn't this increase the excitement?). The breeder may have sent or e-mailed you photos of the puppies they're willing to sell, and your choices will be extremely limited, perhaps between only one or two animals. (Yorkie litters typically consist of just two or three pups.)

While you may want your puppy as young as possible, the breeder may insist that you wait until the pup is 10, 12, or even 16 weeks of age. This allows them to fully assess each pup's potential as either a show or a pet prospect. Show prospects are either kept by the breeder or sold into homes that are prepared to show and eventually breed the dog. Pet homes, on the other hand, are sought for those puppies who appear to be unlikely to succeed as show dogs, often for reasons that you or I would consider insignificant. If you want a wider range of puppies to choose from, you will have to be working with more than one responsible breeder.

Personally, I'm happy to leave the choice of puppy to the breeder. If I've been honest about what I'm looking for (say, a good-looking dog in the six- or seven-pound range, with no congenital defects, a nice, silky coat, and an outgoing temperament), I think the breeder is more able than I to identify such a pup at the tender age of 10 or 12 weeks. And if that breeder is willing to get the pup accustomed to basic handling, grooming, and housetraining, well, I'm not too proud to accept that kind of help. Now that I've already owned a Yorkie, I feel more competent to take on the basics myself, if need be, but a first-time owner would be well-advised to let the breeder select a good pet puppy for them and to get that puppy started on the way to pethood.

The one thing I'd insist on, however, is the choice of male or female. It's hardly rational, but I think the individual preference for a male or a female can be so strong that it probably should not be ignored. Breeders will tell you that their male (or female) Yorkies are less (or more) high-strung, or more affectionate, or easier to train, and they may be right. But if you, as a pet owner, have a powerful preference for one gender over the other, you might as well state it clearly and hold out for a pup of that persuasion because right or wrong, you're more likely to be happy with that choice.

Part II

Caring for Your Yorkshire Terrier

Chapter 5

Bringing Your Yorkshire Terrier Home

You're almost there! Red ink marks the date on the calendar when you get to bring home your brand new puppy. Whether it's your first puppy or just your first Yorkie, this is a time of happy anticipation. It should also be a time of busy preparation.

"What's to prepare?" you ask. Well, would you bring a human baby home without at least a box of diapers and a rattle? A puppy requires at least as much planning as a baby—maybe more. After all, a human baby will stay put for a few months until you figure out what you're doing. A puppy will be all over the place, wreaking havoc, if you're not prepared. To get your puppy off on the right foot, here are some things to line up ahead of time.

Safety Items

You might think the first order of business is food, but unless the Dog Stork drops your puppy down the chimney, you'll have to pick him up somewhere and bring him home. To be safe, the puppy should wear a harness, or a collar and leash, and an ID tag—even if his feet are not expected to touch the ground.

You may be tempted to just slip Mighty Mite into your pocket or place him beside you on the car seat—but *don't.* Invest up front in a secure travel carrier that Mite will come to associate with good times and hop into eagerly whenever you pick up your keys. There are wonderful lightweight canvas shoulder bags on the market that are designed for cats and small dogs (see the appendix). They're perfect for taking your Yorkie shopping or on the bus. Their drawback is that they don't offer the protection of a fiberglass or metal carrier.

You'll find information about the collar, leash, and harness in the box on page 44. As for ID, many a puppy has been tragically lost while his owner was intending to get an identification tag. Avoid this heartbreak by ordering your puppy's tag in advance. If you haven't settled on a name, just use "puppy"; after all, the critical information is your name and telephone numbers (daytime and evening).

Safe Places

Mite will be tiny when you bring him home, but don't wait until you walk through the door with him to consider which areas he'll have access to until he's housetrained or the methods you'll use to keep him there. The critical considerations are that he not be isolated from you any more than necessary, but that he be restricted at first to a small area that can be easily cleaned (no rugs or carpeting). A finished basement, play room, pantry, or laundry room off the kitchen are *not* good ideas. Your puppy needs to be where you are.

Whichever room you choose should be one that can be easily puppy proofed (see the box on page 46). A bright kitchen or even part of a kitchen is ideal for

Puppies with free run of the house will certainly get into trouble.

Puppy Essentials

You'll need to go shopping *before* you bring your puppy home. There are many, many adorable and tempting items at pet supply stores, but these are the basics.

- **Food and water dishes.** Look for bowls that are wide and low or weighted in the bottom so they will be harder to tip over. Stainless steel bowls are a good choice because they are unchewable, easy to clean (plastic never gets completely clean), and almost impossible to break. Beware of hand-painted ceramics or dishes that are not expressly intended for food, as paints may contain lead or other toxic substances. Avoid bowls that place the food and water side by side in one unit—it's too easy for your dog to get his water dirty that way.

- **Leash.** For your puppy's first leash, choose nylon of about the same width as the collar, equipped with a swivel and safety snap. (If you like the look and feel of leather, wait until the puppy is both a little more substantial and is finished teething—roughly 6 months of age.) Most leashes come in four- or six-foot lengths; either is fine for your Yorkie. A retractable lead, which allows your Yorkie to explore roughly sixteen feet away from you, is wonderful when you're walking in parks

the daytime, though you probably will want Mighty Mite to sleep in your room at night (see Crate and Bed, next). Use baby gates to section off a large room or to keep Mite from falling down the cellar stairs. The only drawback to kitchens is that they invariably are full of dangerous cleaning products, ant and roach traps, and other hazards. Protect your Yorkie by figuring out ahead of time how to keep all cupboard doors securely fastened, the contents of the garbage pail or the cat's litter box inaccessible, and Mite himself away from the stove where boiling liquids or spattering grease may land on him.

Crate and Bed

A dog crate (also called a kennel or cage) is the piece of equipment that is going to ensure your puppy is easily housetrained and that he has a place of his own for retreating to when, like Greta Garbo, he "wants to be alone." Some owners or remote places, but most city ordinances require your dog to be on a leash not longer than six feet. Practice with a retractible lead before taking your Yorkie out on the street, and keep in mind that the closer your dog is to you, the safer he is.

- **Collar.** An excellent first collar for a tiny Yorkie puppy is a nylon buckle collar. It's lightweight, inexpensive, and comes in a variety of plain and designer colors. Find the correct size by measuring around the pup's neck, then adding two inches. Expect to replace this collar once or twice as your dog grows; adjustable collars that "grow" with puppies' necks are generally too bulky for a neck as tiny as a Yorkie's.

- **Harness.** An alternative to the collar and leash is a harness and leash. I like harnesses for Yorkies for two reasons: They can't possibly injure the dog's (and especially the puppy's) delicate neck and throat, as collars can; and harnesses can be used to safely lift the entire dog out of harm's way, should that ever be necessary.

- **Crate.** Choose a sturdy crate that is easy to clean and large enough for your puppy to stand up, turn around, and lie down in.

- **Nail cutters.** Get a good, sharp pair that are the appropriate size for the nails you will be cutting. Your dog's breeder or veterinarian can give you some guidance here.

- **Grooming tools.** Different kinds of dogs need different kinds of grooming tools. See chapter 7 for advice on what to buy.

use a crate to housetrain their dog, then replace it later with a "real" dog bed. This is a personal choice, but from the dog's point of view, it's not necessary. If you use the crate correctly, your Yorkie will never want or need another bed.

What's that, you ask? You thought Mighty Mite would just sleep in your bed? Ah, yes, he would like that. But here's the thing to think about: Dogs have a hard enough time learning all the rules of living in a human pack. If the rules keep changing, they are lost. What this means is that you need to think your way past what might seem like a good idea for now, and think instead about life-long habits. So unless you're going to want Mite to sleep with you forever—no matter who else shares the bed, or how old, or sick, or possibly smelly the dog may become due to conditions beyond his control or yours—don't start off that way. A crate set up by your bed will offer all the benefits of having the puppy, and later the dog, close by but will avoid the pitfalls.

Dog crates come in two basic types: the mostly solid fiberglass or molded plastic type approved by airlines and the mostly open wire type. (Canvas carriers

Puppy-Proofing Your Home

You can prevent much of the destruction puppies can cause and keep your new dog safe by looking at your home and yard from a dog's point of view. Get down on all fours and look around. Do you see loose electrical wires, cords dangling from the blinds, or chewy shoes on the floor? Are there gaps and openings small enough for a Yorkie to crawl into and get stuck? Your pup will see them too!

In the kitchen:

- Put all knives and other utensils away in drawers.
- Get a trash can with a tight-fitting lid.
- Put all household cleaners in cupboards that close securely; consider using childproof latches on the cabinet doors.

In the bathroom:

- Keep all household cleaners, medicines, vitamins, shampoos, bath products, perfumes, makeup, nail polish remover, and other personal products in cupboards that close securely; consider using childproof latches on the cabinet doors.
- Get a trash can with a tight-fitting lid.
- Don't use toilet bowl cleaners that release chemicals into the bowl every time you flush.
- Keep the toilet bowl lid down.
- Throw away potpourri and any solid air fresheners.

In the bedroom:

- Securely put away all potentially dangerous items, including medicines and medicine containers, vitamins and supplements, perfumes, and makeup.
- Put all your jewelry, barrettes, and hairpins in secure boxes.
- Pick up all socks, shoes, and other chewables.

are a third possibility. For dogs as small as Yorkies, soft carriers are accepted by some airlines as carry-on luggage and can usually get past security guards and other "dog police.") Molded plastic crates are lightweight and easy to clean.

In the rest of the house:

- Tape up or cover electrical cords; consider childproof covers for unused outlets.
- Knot or tie up any dangling cords from curtains, blinds, and the telephone.
- Securely put away all potentially dangerous items, including medicines and medicine containers, vitamins and supplements, cigarettes, cigars, pipes and pipe tobacco, pens, pencils, felt-tip markers, craft and sewing supplies, and laundry products.
- Put all houseplants out of reach.
- Move breakable items off low tables and shelves.
- Pick up all chewable items, including television and electronics remote controls, cellphones, shoes, socks, slippers and sandals, food, dishes, cups and utensils, toys, books and magazines, and anything else that can be chewed on.

In the garage:

- Store all gardening supplies and pool chemicals out of reach of the dog.
- Store all antifreeze, oil, and other car fluids securely, and clean up any spills by hosing them down for at least ten minutes.
- Put all dangerous substances on high shelves or in cupboards that close securely; consider using childproof latches on the cabinet doors.
- Pick up and put away all tools.
- Sweep the floor for nails and other small, sharp items.

In the yard:

- Put the gardening tools away after each use.
- Make sure the kids put away their toys when they're finished playing.
- Keep the pool covered or otherwise restrict your pup's access to it when you're not there to supervise.
- Secure the cords on backyard lights and other appliances.
- Inspect your fence thoroughly. If there are any gaps or holes in the fence, fix them.
- Make sure you have no toxic plants in the garden.

Wire crates permit air to circulate more readily, enable you to observe the puppy, and enable the puppy to feel less isolated. Place a cuddly cotton blanket or towel in the crate—no synthetics, treated fabrics, or foam.

Dog crates are not inexpensive. Luckily, the smallest size is also the cheapest. The right size will allow your dog, when fully grown, to stand with his head up, turn around, stretch, and sleep comfortably. Bigger than that is not better. If you're thinking of getting two Yorkies and figure you'll just get a larger crate that they can share, forget it. Each Yorkie deserves his own bed, his own private place. Best buddies will be happy to be side by side; they don't need to be on top of each other.

Chews and Toys

Something that's safe and satisfying for a puppy to chew on is more a matter of developmental necessity than the word "toy" suggests. Puppies use their mouths to investigate their environment. In the world of people, however, most of that environment is dangerous or just off-limits to sharp little teeth. That means you must give your puppy (and even your adult dog) something safe and acceptable to chew. To meet Mite's need to chew, the chewies you select should be small enough around to fit into the back of his mouth where the jaw hinges.

Some items sold as chew toys are edible (rawhide, pigs' ears, beef hooves) and some are not (cotton, nylon, vinyl, latex, hard or soft rubber). While you and I know the difference between the two, your puppy may be a little less savvy; inedible objects are eaten by puppies as a matter of course.

Use common sense and natural caution in selecting your puppy's toys. Make sure you get things that won't break or crumble off in little bits, which the dog can choke on. Avoid anything with squeakers or other small parts. Dogs love rawhide bones, but pieces of the rawhide can get caught in your dog's throat, so

Your dog will need a bed and plenty of toys to chew and shake and toss.

they should only be allowed when you are there to supervise. And resign yourself to the fact that all dogs will eventually destroy their toys; as each toy is torn apart, replace it with a new one.

Grooming and Medical Supplies

Grooming is a big part of owning a Yorkie and will be covered in detail in chapter 7. At this point I just want to say that grooming supplies are something you should think about and budget for. Buying at least a few of the basics should be among the things you plan to do before your puppy's arrival. Likewise, there are a number of medical supplies you should purchase and have on hand before you might need them. These are listed in chapter 8. For now, just make a note on your to-do list to set up your grooming and medical supply kits and to be thinking about a convenient and easy-to-find place to store them.

Quality Veterinary Services

Now is also the time to find a veterinarian for your puppy. Resist the temptation to just go to whoever is closest. Ask other dog owners for references, then visit two or three veterinary clinics or hospitals to check them out. Some factors to consider might be whether the clinic provides after-hours or emergency service, how many veterinarians share the practice, and whether they represent different areas of expertise. (Your Yorkie can benefit, for example, from both traditional and more holistic approaches.)

Yorkies are so popular that it's unlikely a veterinarian won't have some in their practice, but ask. You want a doctor who is familiar and comfortable with the special medical issues of the Yorkie. As you're talking to the veterinarian and the receptionist, notice if you feel comfortable.

Your Yorkie will require a considerable commitment from you.

Time and Money

The final items to plan for are time and money. Dogs do take time—always when they're very young, often when they're very old. In the beginning weeks and months, figure that you will be spending at least an hour a day on puppy stuff— handling and grooming, housetraining, teaching basic manners and socializing, preparing food, cleaning up puddles, getting your questions answered, and, of course, cooing and cuddling. Always bring a new puppy home when you can set aside time to get him settled in. A long weekend is the minimum; a few weeks would be ideal. Keep the first few days as calm as possible—no parade of visitors, no excited children, just you and puppy getting to know each other.

Eventually, Yorkie puppy chores will be replaced by adult maintenance routines, but the time requirement will not change much. By the time the puppy has all of his shots and is on a regular walking and exercise schedule, plan to devote ten or fifteen minutes to that schedule, four times a day. The Wee used to walk a minimum of a mile every day, and this kept her in excellent physical condition. Nevertheless, short legs cannot walk a mile as fast as long ones, so it was time that had to be budgeted for. It's true that Yorkies can probably get all the exercise they need running around the house, jumping up and down from the bed or the sofa, but that's a pale substitute for a brisk walk in the wide, fragrant world.

When you're puppy-proofing the house and yard, don't forget about your plants.

As your Yorkie's coat grows, you will need to budget time for grooming; figure an average of ten minutes every day for this task. If you make the mistake of neglecting your daily touch-ups, you will be facing a much larger task on the weekend.

Money is another matter. Dogs typically have high start-up costs, moderate maintenance costs through the bulk of their lives, and then high old-age costs. Although it's no more possible to put a price on the joy and pleasure of a dog than on that of a child, many people fail to remember that responsible dog care does cost money. Time spent budgeting for the near and longer term is time very well spent. You might even want to think about putting some money aside every month for your Yorkie, just as you might for a child. That way you'll always be able to afford the quality of care that a precious companion deserves.

Chapter 6

Feeding Your Yorkshire Terrier

The first commandment of feeding a new puppy or even an adult dog is "Thou shalt make no abrupt changes." Sudden switches in the type or quantity of food, or in water, can bring on stomach upsets and diarrhea, particularly in delicate tummies like your Yorkie's. So the first thing to do is find out what kind and amount of food the puppy has been eating and get about a week's supply. If you do intend to switch to a different food, make the changeover gradually by mixing the new and old foods together during the course of a week.

If you pick your puppy up from a breeder, ask for a bottle of the water the puppy is used to, and make a gradual changeover in your water too. (There are many good reasons to obtain your puppy from a conscientious breeder. That person's willingness to help your puppy make a smooth transition into your home is one of them.)

So much for rules. Here are some other things to think about in regard to food and feeding.

Choices, Choices

There are almost too many food choices available to today's dog owner. It can make you think there must be a single best food or combination of foods for your Yorkie, and that it's your job to figure out what that one perfect food is. Not so. Your Yorkie will probably do well on most commercial diets. Make sure any food you buy is specifically for dogs and that it carries the words "complete and balanced" or "nutritionally complete" on the label. (See page 54 for more about reading dog food labels.)

Many Yorkie specialists feed one brand of food exclusively when it works well for them. That approach has its attractions. However, my feeling is that the Yorkie who is fed many different foods is less likely to become finicky or to suffer digestive upsets if you have to change her diet for some reason.

Try to relax about mealtimes. Yorkies are good eaters unless they are allowed to become fusspots. Incidentally, if I overdo the advice to relax, it's because I was unable to follow that advice when The Wee was a wee thing. If you've never had a puppy as tiny as a Yorkie, it can be hard to believe they aren't desperately delicate. They aren't, as long as you avoid puppies advertised as "teacups" or "miniatures" (there are no such classifications of Yorkies) and puppies younger than about 10 weeks.

Dry or Canned Food?

This is really a matter of choice. Some Yorkies prefer one, some the other; most will eat both if they're fed both. Dry food helps clean tartar from the teeth, but because it has no moisture, puppies who eat only dry food will drink a lot of water. This can complicate housetraining. For this reason, I recommend feeding canned food until your puppy is housetrained.

Ages and Stages

Most name-brand dog food manufacturers now offer products for the major stages of a dog's life: puppy, adult, senior, high performance, and low calorie.

Different dogs may do best on different diets.

Reading Dog Food Labels

Dog food labels are not always easy to read, but if you know what to look for they can tell you a lot about what your dog is eating.

- The label should have a statement saying the dog food meets or exceeds the American Association of Feed Control Officials (AAFCO) nutritional guidelines. If the dog food doesn't meet AAFCO guidelines, it can't be considered complete and balanced, and can cause nutritional deficiencies.
- The guaranteed analysis lists the minimum percentages of crude protein and crude fat and the maximum percentages of crude fiber and water. AAFCO requires a minimum of 18 percent crude protein for adult dogs and 22 percent crude protein for puppies on a dry matter basis (that means with the water removed; canned foods should have more protein because they have more water). Dog food must also have a minimum of 5 percent crude fat for adults and 8 percent crude fat for puppies.
- The ingredients list the most common item in the food first, and so on until you get to the least common item, which is listed last.
- Look for a dog food that lists an animal protein source first, such as chicken or poultry meal, beef or beef byproducts, and that has other protein sources listed among the top five ingredients. That's because a food that lists chicken, wheat, wheat gluten, corn, and wheat fiber as the first five ingredients has more chicken than wheat, but may not have more chicken than all the grain products put together.
- Other ingredients may include a carbohydrate source, fat, vitamins and minerals, preservatives, fiber, and sometimes other additives purported to be healthy.
- Some grocery store brands may add artificial colors, sugar, and fillers—all of which should be avoided.

Dogs who lived and died before these foods were available did just fine without them, but why not take advantage? Puppies do need extra protein and fat as they grow, and most breeders recommend keeping a dog on puppy or growth food until she is 1 year old. Again, keep a relaxed attitude. If you run out of puppy food, it's not going to hurt to feed your dog something else for a day or two.

Natural and Organic

Organically grown natural foods are becoming more and more popular for people and for pets. Organically grown foods and meats have been produced without pesticides, hormones, and antibiotics, which add nothing beneficial to the food and can be harmful.

Ingredients you don't want to see are meat, animal, or poultry by-product *meal*, which may contain up to 14 percent indigestible materials. (It's a common misconception that animal by-products are bad food. Generally, they are the clean parts of the animal that are not muscle meat. They do not contain hair, feathers, horns, teeth, hooves, hide, or stomach contents.) You also don't want to see additions such as artificial colors or flavorings, sweeteners, or sugars.

The question of preservatives is less easily answered. Ideally, you could do without them, but this choice requires vigilant attention to shelf life. It also means you must feel confident that your shopkeeper is careful about the conditions under which products are shipped and kept in the store. The best of all possible situations would be if your Yorkie's food (and your own) could be grown organically in the next town and delivered fresh to your doorstep. Until that day arrives, however, be assured that, in most cases, your Yorkie can safely eat from the pet supply store shelf.

For a longhaired dog like the Yorkie, nutrition plays a key role in maintaining that luxurious, shiny coat.

Pet Food vs. People Food

Many of the foods we eat are excellent sources of nutrients—after all, we do just fine on them. But dogs, just like us, need the right combination of meat and other ingredients for a complete and balanced diet, and a bowl of meat doesn't provide that. In the wild, dogs eat the fur, skin, bones, and guts of their prey, and even the contents of the stomach.

This doesn't mean your dog can't eat what you eat. A little meat, dairy, bread, some fruits, or vegetables as a treat are great. Fresh foods have natural enzymes that processed foods don't have. Just remember, we're talking about the same food you eat, not the gristly, greasy leftovers you would normally toss in the trash. Stay away from sugar, too, and remember that chocolate is toxic to dogs.

If you want to share your food with your dog, be sure the total amount you give her each day doesn't make up more than 15 percent of her diet, and that the rest of what you feed her is a top-quality complete and balanced dog food. (More people food could upset the balance of nutrients in the commercial food.)

Can your dog eat an entirely homemade diet? Certainly, if you are willing to work at it. Any homemade diet will have to be carefully balanced, with all the right nutrients in just the right amounts. It requires a lot of research to make a proper home-made diet, but it can be done. It's best to work with a veterinary nutritionist.

How Much and How Often

The chart on page 57 gives you some guidelines for how often to feed your growing puppy. Once she is 18 weeks old, the Yorkie should remain on two meals a day for life. It is too much work for her digestive system to take in and process enough food at one meal to meet her energy needs for an entire day.

There's a fairly simple formula for figuring out how often to feed your puppy, based on her age:

How Many Meals?

Age	Meals per Day	Meal Times
8 to 12 weeks	4	Morning, early afternoon, early evening, before bedtime
12 to 18 weeks	3	Morning, early evening, before bedtime
Over 18 weeks	2	Morning, early evening

There is also an easy formula for the amount to feed your Yorkie. Figure one tablespoon of food per meal for each pound the Yorkie weighs. Thus, a one-pound puppy needs one tablespoon of food at each meal. If the puppy weighs four pounds, she will need approximately four tablespoons of food per meal—though she will be eating fewer times a day.

Keep in mind that these are rough estimates. Your puppy may need a little more or a little less. Guidelines are only that—your best guide to how much to feed your Yorkie is your Yorkie. If she leaves food in her dish, she needs that much less. If she cleans her bowl and still seems hungry, offer just a tiny bit more. And once again, try to relax. A puppy this age probably won't overeat, and if one or two meals are a little skimpy, the world won't end.

Snacks and Treats

Once your puppy is doing well on a regular feeding schedule, you can offer her occasional snacks if there's some reason to do so. For instance, if you take an especially long walk one day, or if the puppy plays more vigorously than usual or has a particularly exciting morning romping with a friend, a snack makes sense; the puppy probably could use a little energy boost.

Treats, on the other hand, are best reserved as training aides. A food lure or treat is an effective way

Feeding your dog from the table will only encourage more begging. Right from the start, make it clear that when you're eating, your dog is not.

to help your puppy or dog to learn new behaviors or to reinforce behavior you want the puppy to retain. Very small pieces of cheese or some other nutritious food with a strong aroma make perfect training treats. Offering treats at random times and for no apparent reason diminishes their effectiveness as training tools.

Keep in mind that both snacks and treats are still food. The calories of any snacks and treats offered during the day must be calculated and subtracted from the day's overall ration. If you neglect to do this for long, you will find your Yorkie is starting to get thick. Excess weight in dogs creates the same problems as it does in people!

Feeding Do's and Don'ts

Following a few simple feeding guidelines will help you make sure your Yorkie stays in good health and physical condition. Once the dog has settled into your home and feels comfortable, you can experiment with different foods to see what your Yorkie likes. Keep in mind that this experimentation should not be overly abrupt. While you do this, keep a food diary so that you can monitor what happens when you offer different foods and varying amounts.

Pick a quiet, out-of-the-way spot for your Yorkie to eat, and be sure to schedule her meals for the same times every day. Doing this will help to establish good eating and elimination habits. Keeping to a schedule means that you have to keep your own eating schedule fairly regular as well; it's definitely a good idea to feed your Yorkie after you eat—dogs understand that leaders eat first. As for snacks, if you do decide to give them to your Yorkie periodically, try to make them nutritious. Whole foods such as bits of raw carrots, green beans, apples, or bananas are good examples.

When it comes to feeding your Yorkie, there are just as many things you shouldn't do as there are things you should. Again, don't switch food or water abruptly, and don't leave food down any longer than ten or fifteen minutes. If the dog clearly has an aversion to a particular flavor or brand of food, don't buy it again. You should also discontinue feeding your Yorkie a particular food if you find that it gives her gas or causes a loose or hard, dry stool. Don't feed her generic dog foods; raw or undercooked pork, fish, or seafood; and definitely avoid milk, onions (raw or cooked), and especially chocolate.

Along with love and consistency and exercise, providing good food is one of the important things that you do for your Yorkie. The neat thing about nutrition is that food and feeding has visible outcomes: You aren't going to over-, under-, or misfeed your Yorkie for long without seeing the telltale signs. You can be reasonably sure you're hitting the nutritional mark as long as your Yorkie has clear skin and eyes, a shiny coat with ribs you can feel beneath it, high spirits and good weight, and well-formed stools that are easy to pick up.

Chapter 7

Grooming Your Yorkshire Terrier

I t's wonderful that life offers so many options, but sometimes it's easier when there's only one right answer. That's the way it is with grooming the Yorkshire Terrier: *It has to be done.* It doesn't matter whether your Yorkie's coat is stupendous, superb, satisfactory, or only so-so—he still has to be groomed. This, however, really is good news. Grooming Samson is one of the best ways there is to get to know him intimately, to detect health problems such as lumps, rashes, fleas, and ticks, and it will become a soothing ritual for you both—provided you get off on the right foot.

Begin at . . . the Beginning

If you acquired Samson from a conscientious breeder, undoubtedly he's already been introduced to the basics of being groomed: a little light brushing, having his nails clipped, a bit of scissoring around his ears and feet, maybe even his first bath. Whatever the breeder did or didn't do, the most important thing was gently initiating the puppy at a very early age to procedures that will become as much a part of his life as eating.

So if Samson has had this exposure, you're ahead of the game. If he hasn't, the time for you to start is right now. It doesn't matter that his coat is only an inch long; it's his attitude that you're "grooming" at this point. His acceptance, your skills and confidence, and his coat will all grow together.

You don't need a lot of fancy supplies to care for your Yorkie—in the beginning or ever. Down the road, if you find yourself really getting into the grooming thing, you may want to invest in additional supplies. For now, the items in the box on page 60 should suffice.

Setting Up a Routine

Just as with feeding, walking, training, and everything else, you will want to establish a routine for grooming that your puppy can learn to depend on. The sequence I recommend is brush, comb, trim, bathe, cut nails, blow dry.

But first, where will you do the grooming? Some people train their Yorkie to lie in their lap or on a table for grooming, turning the body from side to side as necessary. Others groom with the dog standing on a stool, table, or countertop. I find there's less strain on my back if I can sit or stand and have the dog roughly at waist height. The obvious and very real danger in this is that if your puppy is standing on a table, you cannot take your eyes or hands off him for one single second. Don't even wonder whether Samson will jump—he will!

Grooming Supplies

Pin or bristle brush

Comb

Flea comb or very fine-toothed comb

Electric razor

Safety scissors

Small dog nail trimmer

Gauze (for cleaning teeth)

Ear powder

Pet shampoo

Pet coat conditioner

Rubber mat

Sponge

Spray attachment for the faucet

Cotton balls

Towels

Hair dryer

Small rubber bands

Bows or barrettes (optional)

Once you've decided on a location, gather together all your supplies so you can proceed in an orderly way. I wouldn't attempt a full-scale grooming session on a new dog for several weeks. It will pay off in the long run if you start slowly, spend just a few seconds on each maneuver, and concentrate on following the same sequence each time. For instance, first you might run the brush gently over the puppy's legs, body, and head, all in ten seconds, then go over the same areas, in the same order, with the comb, in another ten seconds. As you work, talk softly and calmly to the puppy. You don't want to wheedle or plead with him to stand still (out of the question anyway!), nor do you want to get gruff or impatient. If you explain to him what you're doing and why, regardless of the fact that he won't understand a single word, you will have automatically adopted the right no-nonsense tone.

Only regular grooming will keep your dog's coat in condition. Get him used to brushing and combing when he's young to avoid any later fussing.

How to Brush and Comb Your Yorkie

If you grew up in the 1950s, as I did, you brushed your hair a hundred strokes a day because your mother said doing so was good for your scalp and would make your hair shine. Then you combed your hair to get out the tangles, to put in a part, or maybe to draw it all up into a glossy pony-tail. Obviously, hair-care strategies for humans have changed dramatically since then. But when it comes to your Yorkie, it's back to the 1950s. If you choose to do only one part of a full grooming routine on your Yorkie, make faithful and thorough brushing and combing your choice.

> **TIP**
>
> Don't give Samson a chewie or toy to distract him while you groom. He really does have to learn that this is a serious time. Praise him calmly for every few seconds that he is calm and cooperative. And don't ever let him convince you to put down the comb, brush, or clippers when *he* says so; that only teaches him that if he squirms and struggles, you'll stop.

Brushing your dog on a table will save your back.

Brush first. This separates the hair, distributes the skin's natural oils, and feels good. Then, with short downward strokes, comb slowly and carefully. Begin near the tips of the hair and work your way toward the dog's body, feeling for tangles or small matted areas. If you encounter resistance, stop. The smallest tug against a tangle will elicit a piercing yip from your Yorkie that neither of you will soon forget. You don't need that!

Grasp the problem area with your fingers, lifting the coat to make sure you release any tension against the dog's skin. Then break up the mats using your fingers, the brush, or the tip of the comb. Only when you can comb cleanly through the area that was snarled or matted should you release your grip on the coat and comb from the skin outward.

When you're through combing Samson, the comb should run through smoothly, from the skin to the tips of the hair, just as it does in your own hair. Not just down the center of his back, but everywhere: in the armpits, on the insides of the rear legs, behind the ears, on the tops of the feet, at the corners of the mouth. If Samson is a puppy whose coat is just beginning to grow, you shouldn't encounter anything too serious, although eating and drinking can gum up the hair around the mouth, and stepping in puddles of urine can cause the hair on the rear feet to mat. During your first grooming sessions, tackle one small tangle at a time, then move on.

How to Trim Your Yorkie

There's not much trimming to be done on a Yorkie, and until the hair gets a little longer, you may be snipping air. Still, it's important for both of you to get used to the feel and sound of the scissors. Later on, you may decide you like the look of a puppy trim, which just means keeping the body coat short and cutting in "bangs" on the forehead. You probably will want to have a professional groomer give your dog his first puppy trim. After that, you can just follow the outline as the coat grows out.

How Often?

A stitch in time saves nine, and keeping your Yorkie's coat clean and mat free is so much easier than trying to correct a neglected coat a month later. Here's the schedule I recommend:

Brushing and combing—every single day
Cleaning the beard and under the eyes—every day
Clipping nails—once a week
Bathing—once a month or as needed

Start with the dog's feet. Stand the Yorkie on a table and trim all the way around the top outline of each foot. When he lifts the foot you're working on (and he will, because dogs are sensitive around their feet), lift the opposite foot instead and hold it up—this will force him to stand on the one you're trimming. Then lift each foot, place the scissors flat against the foot pad, and snip all hair flush with the foot pad. (Be careful not to pinch the pad with the scissors.) Again, end this step when he's standing quietly, not when he's resisting.

Next come the ears. Using a man's electric mustache trimmer, remove the hair on both sides of the tip of the ear (roughly the top one-quarter or one-third). Then scissor around the ear tip. Don't worry about getting right up to the edge until you're more comfortable using the scissors. Your Yorkie will be wiggling and tossing his head, but don't try to forcibly restrain him. Concentrate on holding the ear gently but firmly, talking calmly, and going through the motions until he figures out this isn't going to hurt.

You'll need to trim the excess hair in your dog's ears and on his feet. You may also want to shorten his coat to keep it from dragging on the ground.

Your Yorkie will stay cleaner longer if you get in the habit of cutting away the long hair that grows around the rectum and genital areas. Practice the motions before you actually cut any hair. Scissoring the genital area is easiest with the dog lying on his back in your lap. Rest one hand on the puppy to steady him— Yorkies are famous for sudden moves.

How to Bathe Your Yorkie

Never immerse your dog in water; use a gentle spray to wet and rinse him.

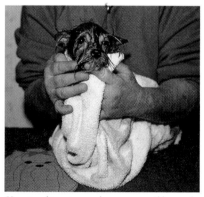

Use a towel to get as much water as possible out of the dog's coat.

Bathe your Yorkie in a warm room, away from drafts. Puppy's first baths will be stressful, so pick a day when nothing else is going on and when the puppy is feeling and eating well. After his bath, your puppy will probably need to urinate and then will want to be left alone for a nice, long rest.

Place a nonslip mat in the sink, then cut a hole in the portion that covers the drain so the water can run out. Attach the sprayer to the faucet and experiment until the water temperature is warm and the flow is light to moderate. Put small plugs of cotton in each of your Yorkie's ears, then stand him on the mat in the sink and reassure him for a minute.

Thoroughly wet the coat and the underside of the dog. Use the sponge to wet his head and face. Shampoo the body, add a bit more water, and use your fingers to work up a lather. (Don't rub the coat in circles.) Wash down each leg and under the feet. Wash the head last by applying the shampoo to the sponge. Try to avoid getting shampoo in the eyes or mouth. Then rinse the whole dog thoroughly, first the head, then the body and legs, then underneath. Make sure every speck of shampoo is out of the coat and off the skin.

Place the puppy on one towel and dry him gently with the other, squeezing as much water as possible into the towel. (Don't squeeze the dog! Use the towel to gather up bunches of hair that you can squeeze dry.) At this point, The Wee always wanted to get down on the floor and tear around for a minute or two, growling and barking and wiping her whole body on the carpet, bedspread, or slipcovers. Then I would scoop her up again and dry her with the hair dryer (not too hot and not too close to the skin), brushing her coat as it dried.

How to Clip Your Yorkie's Nails

Nails can be clipped when they're dry, but dogs seem to mind it less when they're soft from the bath. Unless your Yorkie is truly angelic, begin by just doing one or two nails at a time, and take off only the tiny bit that curves down at the tip (when the nail is viewed from the side or underside). Yorkies' nails are black, and you won't be able to see the vein or quick inside; this vein does not extend past the curved portion of the nail, but it will bleed if you nick it. It will hurt, and your

Regular nail clipping is important for the health of your dog's feet. Start your Yorkie on a regular routine, and it won't turn into a wrestling match.

Yorkie will never forget it. As with other grooming procedures, praise the dog for cooperative behavior, and don't let him think that if he resists, you'll desist.

Fleas and Ticks

Fleas have been a common and troublesome enemy of dogs for centuries. They are usually spotted first during a grooming session, which is why they are mentioned here. In fact, regular bathing and brushing will help prevent infestations and enable you to catch the first little flea before it becomes the parent to thousands.

You should take steps to prevent your Yorkie from becoming host to these blood suckers. Don't, however, go overboard. A chemical strong enough to kill fleas and ticks is potentially dangerous to your dog as well. When misused, overused, and combined with others, these products can be worse for your dog than the pests themselves. Here are some tips for prevention:

- Keep your dog in maximum good health. Healthy dogs with strong immune systems are able to repel pests naturally.
- Avoid close contact with other dogs or outdoor cats. Fleas can easily jump from one animal to another.
- Learn when pests are in full force where you live. Avoid sandy, grassy, and wooded areas during flea and tick season.

Once you've got the problem, you have to get rid of it. The box on page 67 describes the relatively new products on the market that often solve the average flea problem completely. These are products you get from a veterinarian, so be sure to ask your vet about them. Even though these products are highly successful in eliminating fleas, it is wise to be vigilant.

Fleas and ticks lurk everywhere—even in urban parks—and you must examine your dog regularly for signs of these parasites.

The seriousness of both flea and tick infestations should not be underestimated. A large number of fleas can actually kill a dog, especially one who is very young or very old. Each time one of these pests bites your Yorkie, it ingests a drop or two of blood. When your dog is covered by hundreds of fleas, each of which bites him numerous times a day, the blood loss can actually be quite substantial. In addition, fleas can cause skin allergies and are the intermediary hosts of tapeworms, an internal parasite (see chapter 8).

New Products in the Fight Against Fleas

At one time, battling fleas meant exposing your dog and yourself to toxic dips, sprays, powders, and collars. But today there are flea preventives that work very well and are safe for your dog, you, and the environment. The two most common types are insect growth regulators (IGRs), which stop the immature flea from developing or maturing, and adult flea killers. To deal with an active infestation, experts usually recommend a product that has both.

These next-generation flea fighters generally come in one of two forms.

- **Topical treatments or spot-ons.** These products are applied to the skin, usually between the shoulder blades. The product is absorbed through the skin into the dog's system. Among the most widely available spot-ons are Advantage (kills adult fleas and larvae), Revolution (kills adult fleas), Frontline Plus (kills adult fleas and larvae, plus an IGR), K-9 Advantix (kills adult fleas and larvae), and BioSpot (kills adult fleas and larvae, plus an IGR).
- **Systemic products.** This is a pill your dog swallows that transmits a chemical throughout the dog's bloodstream. When a flea bites the dog, it picks up this chemical, which then prevents the flea's eggs from developing. Among the most widely available systemic products are Program (kills larvae only, plus an IGR) and Capstar (kills adult fleas).

Make sure you read all the labels and apply the products exactly as recommended, and that you check to make sure they are safe for puppies.

Making Your Environment Flea Free

If there are fleas on your dog, there are fleas in your home, yard, and car, even if you can't see them. Take these steps to combat them.

In your home:

- Wash whatever is washable (the dog bed, sheets, blankets, pillow covers, slipcovers, curtains, etc.).
- Vacuum everything else in your home—furniture, floors, rugs, everything. Pay special attention to the folds and crevices in upholstery, cracks between floorboards, and the spaces between the floor and the baseboards. Flea larvae are sensitive to sunlight, so inside the house they prefer deep carpet, bedding, and cracks and crevices.
- When you're done, throw the vacuum cleaner bag away—in an outside garbage can.
- Use a nontoxic flea-killing powder, such as Flea Busters or Zodiac FleaTrol, to treat your carpets (but remember, it does not control fleas elsewhere in the house). The powder stays deep in the carpet and kills fleas (using a form of boric acid) for up to a year.
- If you have a particularly serious flea problem, consider using a fogger or long-lasting spray to kill any adult and larval fleas, or having a professional exterminator treat your home.

How to Get Rid of a Tick

You should inspect your Yorkie thoroughly for ticks, especially where they tend to collect: in the ears, in the hair at the base of the ears, in the armpits, and around the genitals.

Although Frontline, K-9 Advantix, and BioSpot, the new generation of flea fighters, are partially effective in killing ticks once they are on your dog, they are not 100 percent effective and will not keep ticks from biting your dog in the first place. During tick season (which, depending on where you live, can be spring, summer, and/or fall), examine your dog every day for ticks. Pay particular attention to your dog's neck, behind the ears, the armpits, and the groin.

In your car:

- Take out the floor mats and hose them down with a strong stream of water, then hang them up to dry in the sun.
- Wash any towels, blankets, or other bedding you regularly keep in the car.
- Thoroughly vacuum the entire interior of your car, paying special attention to the seams between the bottom and back of the seats.
- When you're done, throw the vacuum cleaner bag away—in an outside garbage can.

In your yard:

- Flea larvae prefer shaded areas that have plenty of organic material and moisture, so rake the yard thoroughly and bag all the debris in tightly sealed bags.
- Spray your yard with an insecticide that has residual activity for at least thirty days. Insecticides that use a form of boric acid are nontoxic. Some newer products contain an insect growth regulator (such as fenoxycarb) and need to be applied only once or twice a year.
- For an especially difficult flea problem, consider having an exterminator treat your yard.
- Keep your yard free of piles of leaves, weeds, and other organic debris. Be especially careful in shady, moist areas, such as under bushes.

When you find a tick, use a pair of tweezers to grasp the tick as close as possible to the dog's skin and pull it out using firm, steady pressure. Check to make sure you get the whole tick (mouth parts left in your dog's skin can cause an infection), then dab the wound with a little hydrogen peroxide and some antibiotic ointment. Watch for signs of inflammation.

Ticks carry very serious diseases that are transmittable to humans, so dispose of the tick safely. *Never* crush it between your fingers. Don't flush it down the toilet either, because the tick will survive the trip and infect another animal. Instead, use the tweezers to place the tick in a tight-sealing jar or plastic dish with a little alcohol, put on the lid and dispose of the container in an outdoor garbage can. Wash the tweezers thoroughly with hot water and alcohol.

Finishing Touches

According to the breed standard, Yorkies' coats are parted on the top of the muzzle and from the back of the skull to the end of the tail. Later, you may decide you don't want to be bothered with this, but until then, why not give it a whirl?

As soon as your puppy has enough hair for a topknot, comb it up and fasten it in a rubber band or in some kind of clasp. Make sure the hair isn't pulled too tight and that you don't accidentally catch any skin in the rubber band. Small ribbons, bits of yarn, or baby barrettes can be added if you like.

Chapter 8

Keeping Your Yorkshire Terrier Healthy

I f "a stitch in time saves nine" is the key to keeping your Yorkie well-groomed, the key to keeping her healthy is "an ounce of prevention is worth a pound of cure." This approach to veterinary care parallels current trends in human medicine and makes perfect sense in both. With so much emphasis on wellness and well-being, it's an exciting time to be getting a new puppy.

Preventive Veterinary Care

A day or so after you get your new puppy is a good time to visit the veterinarian for Lamb Chop's first exam. Take along a stool sample to be tested for internal parasites. Also take along some kind of notebook that will become Lamb Chop's very own record book, and get in the habit of entering information on the spot.

Ask questions. For example, if the vet takes Lamb Chop's temperature, ask them what it is, and write it down. If they note a little clicking in the right rear knee, write that down, too. It's all well and good for this data to be in the clinic's files, but it's nice to have your own independent file on your dog. Busy vets will not review your dog's entire file each time you visit, but you can, and you can ask the vet to recheck anything you're concerned about.

Vaccines

What vaccines dogs need and how often they need them has been a subject of controversy for several years. Researchers, health care professionals, vaccine manufacturers, and dog owners do not always agree on which vaccines each dog needs or how often booster shots must be given.

In 2003, the American Animal Hospital Association released vaccination guidelines and recommendations that have helped dog owners and veterinarians sort through much of the controversy and conflicting information. The guidelines designate four vaccines as core, or essential, because of the serious nature of the diseases and their widespread distribution. These are canine distemper virus, canine parvovirus, canine adenovirus-2, and rabies. The general recommendations for their use (except rabies, for which you must follow local laws) are:

- Vaccinate puppies at 6–8 weeks, 9–11 weeks, and 12–14 weeks.
- Give a booster shot when the dog is 1 year old.

Lamb Chop is bound to respond more positively to her new doctor if no vaccinations are given on her first visit. Many veterinarians keep tasty treats on hand to help their patients feel less fearful in the future; in case yours doesn't, take something along in your pocket and ask the veterinarian to give it to your puppy.

Puppy Preventive Care

Review with your veterinarian the types of vaccines your puppy has had, as this will determine when the next series is due. Some Yorkie breeders prefer not to give permanent vaccines to Yorkie puppies before the age of 3 months. Others feel vaccines should be given for one disease at a time rather than in an all-in-one shot, which they fear may overwhelm the puppy's immune system. The

- Give a subsequent booster shot every three years, unless there are risk factors that make it necessary to vaccinate more or less often.

Noncore vaccines should only be considered for those dogs who risk exposure to a particular disease because of geographic area, lifestyle, frequency of travel, or other issues. They include vaccines against distemper-measles virus, canine parainfluenza virus, leptospirosis, Bordetella bronchiseptica, and Borrelia burgdorferi (Lyme disease).

Vaccines that are not generally recommended because the disease poses little risk to dogs or is easily treatable, or the vaccine has not been proven to be effective, are those against Giardia, canine coronavirus, and canine adenovirus-1.

Often, combination injections are given to puppies, with one shot containing several core and noncore vaccines. Your veterinarian may be reluctant to use separate shots that do not include the noncore vaccines, because they must be specially ordered. If you are concerned about these noncore vaccines, talk to your vet.

three-year rabies vaccine, normally given at 3 months of age, is generally considered too painful for Yorkshire Terriers, so ask instead for the one-year vaccine. A new three-year distemper vaccine just became available in 2004. Just make sure that a three-year vaccine doesn't tempt you to avoid annual veterinary checkups. In any case, remember that until Lamb Chop is fully immunized, you must keep her away from areas where other dogs have been walked (that is, where urine and feces have been deposited).

Other subjects to discuss with your veterinarian at your first visit are any local veterinary issues you should be aware of, such as whether you need to be concerned about heartworm or Lyme disease. Ask the vet to demonstrate any procedure you're unsure about, such as how much nail to clip off, how to take the puppy's temperature, or how to open her mouth for inspection. If the

Toy dogs are not the same as the big breeds, behaviorally or physiologically. Try to find a veterinarian who has experience treating small dogs.

veterinarian does not provide emergency care, find out which emergency clinic they use. Enter this information in the record book too.

Adult Preventive Care

After your puppy is fully immunized, you may not see the veterinarian again for a year. In all likelihood, you will receive reminders when Lamb Chop is due for follow-up visits. Normally this is done annually, but depending on where you live and what your dog is exposed to, a different schedule may be recommended. The following are the usual items on the annual visit checklist.

Physical Exam

The vet will check eyes, ears, mouth, heart and lungs, skin and coat, and palpate internal organs. My vet's office is too small for the doctor to be able to watch even a Yorkie walk back and forth, but watching your dog move should be a part of her physical exam. Bring any changes you've noticed to the vet's attention. If Lamb Chop has always jumped up on the sofa to harass birds outside the window but doesn't seem to bother with them anymore, bring this up. Changes in behavior are the best clues we have that something may be bothering our small friends.

Vaccination Boosters

If your dog is on a three-year vaccination schedule, you may want to give the various shots in alternating years to avoiding overloading Lamb Chop's immune system. And all vaccines, even rabies (which is the only one required by law), can be waived for a dog who isn't in good health.

Stool Sample

There are a number of different kinds of parasites that your dog can pick up (see "Internal Parasites" on page 87), mostly by ingesting their eggs when eating such things as uncooked meat or fish, contaminated soil, infested animal droppings, or fleas. Routine worming is not recommended. Even a positive finding in the stool does not always mean a dog needs to be treated if she does not appear to be ill in any way. Puppies are much more likely to be made ill by internal parasites; healthy adults often can fight them off.

Heartworm Prevention

Anywhere there are mosquitoes, your dog is at risk for getting heartworms. This risk is serious; heartworms can be fatal. Preventing heartworms with a once-a-month tablet is much easier and safer than treating a dog for the disease.

Your veterinarian should be a resource for you for the life of your dog. Ask questions and take notes.

Why Spay and Neuter?

Breeding dogs is a serious undertaking that should only be part of a well-planned breeding program. Why? Because dogs pass on their physical and behavioral problems to their offspring. Even healthy, well-behaved dogs can pass on problems in their genes.

Is your dog so sweet that you'd like to have a litter of puppies just like her? If you breed her to another dog, the pups will not have the same genetic heritage she has. Breeding her *parents* again will increase the odds of a similar pup, but even then, the puppies in the second litter could inherit different genes. In fact, *there is no way to breed a dog to be just like another dog.*

Meanwhile, thousands and thousands of dogs are killed in animal shelters every year simply because they have no homes. Casual breeding is a big contributor to this problem.

If you don't plan to breed your dog, is it still a good idea to spay her or neuter him? Yes!

Although the likelihood of being bitten by an infected mosquito is a seasonal concern in most parts of the country, many veterinarians are now recommending that dogs stay on heartworm preventives yearlong because it prevents other kinds of worms as well, including some that are contagious to humans. (Personally, I've lived long enough to be skeptical of any drug that's presumed perfectly safe and innocuous for anyone to take forever.) If you choose not to do this, you will need to have your dog's blood rechecked each year before mosquito season begins. This is because it is dangerous for your dog to receive heartworm preventive if she is already harboring the worms.

Special Preventive Care: Spay/Neuter

Spaying your female Yorkie or neutering your male is heavy-duty prevention. In addition to absolutely preventing innocent puppies from being born with

When you spay your female:

- You avoid her heat cycles, during which she discharges blood and scent.
- It greatly reduces the risk of mammary cancer and eliminates the risk of pyometra (an often fatal infection of the uterus) and uterine cancer.
- It prevents unwanted pregnancies.
- It reduces dominance behaviors and aggression.

When you neuter your male:

- It curbs the desire to roam and to fight with other males.
- It greatly reduces the risk of prostate cancer and eliminates the risk of testicular cancer.
- It helps reduce leg lifting and mounting behavior.
- It reduces dominance behaviors and aggression.

possible genetic diseases you'd have no way of anticipating, there are a number of diseases, conditions, and behaviors you can either prevent or improve the odds against (see the box on page 76).

Geriatric Preventive Care

Most dogs are considered seniors after they turn 7; for Yorkies, however, this may turn out to be only early middle age. My veterinarian offers a geriatric preventive exam for dogs over 7. This includes a urinalysis and complete blood count to screen for various factors and pick up problems that might be developing. Depending on the results, further specific tests for heart, lungs, liver, or kidneys might be ordered. The geriatric preventive exam gives the veterinarian a baseline against which to compare future tests. If your vet doesn't offer such a program, why not ask about it?

Know Your Yorkie

As the owner of a treasured Yorkie, you can and should feel like a full partner with your veterinarian in maintaining your Yorkie's health and well-being. One way to do this is by making it a point to know what's normal for your dog so that you'll immediately know when something is not quite right. Even if the information does nothing more than generate a phone call to your veterinarian, often that's enough. In addition to your dog's daily massage and check, here are some things you can do.

Know Your Yorkie's Vital Signs

Temperature

The normal average temperature for dogs is 101.3 degrees Fahrenheit, although your own dog's normal temperature may be as low as 100 or as high as 102.5. Don't rely too much on the temperature (or other vital readings) from the veterinarian's office, as the stress of being there can cause changes. Take your dog's temperature at home from time to time, when all is normal, and record it in your dog's record book. By occasionally practicing this skill, your confidence will grow.

Know your Yorkie's normal vital signs so you can better gauge when something is wrong.

Whenever you suspect your Yorkie's not well, the first thing to do is find out if she has a fever. Being able to relay this information to your veterinarian or an emergency clinic will help them assess the situation.

To take your Yorkie's temperature, use an infant's rectal thermometer (make sure it's calibrated to the Fahrenheit scale) or a digital thermometer. Follow the manufacturer's instructions for lubrication, then lift and firmly hold your dog's tail so she can't sit down, and gently insert the bulb end into the rectum as directed, using a slow, steady, twisting motion. Hold the thermometer in place for as long as directed, remove it, and read the findings.

Pulse

A normal resting pulse for dogs is between 70 and 130 beats per minute. Toy dogs tend to have faster pulses, but certain well-conditioned, athletic dogs in this group do have slower ones.

To take your Yorkie's pulse, have the dog stand while you run your fingers along the inside of one of the

When you know what is normal for your dog, you will also know when something is not quite right.

back thighs and stop where the leg attaches to the body. Press firmly with your fingers to feel the pulsation and count the number of beats in a minute. (Use a watch with a second hand.) You can also try to take the pulse over the heart on the left side of the chest, but with all that panting and snuffling in your face, it will probably be harder to do.

Respiration

A normal respiration rate is ten to thirty breaths a minute, at rest. Just watch the rise and fall of your Yorkie's chest when she's lying quietly but not in a deep sleep.

Appetite

Notice your dog's normal appetite, how much she eats and how fast, as well as what affects her appetite (excitement, thunderstorms, company, being in an unfamiliar place). There's no right or wrong; what's important is to know what's normal for your dog.

Elimination Habits

Make a point of noticing your dog's regular bowel and urinary habits. What's the frequency? The quantity, consistency, color? Any change in either is a sign to be looked into.

Changes in your dog's behavior could signal a health problem.

Behavior

Changes in your Yorkie's behavior (when Sweetie Pie suddenly snaps or Joe Kool starts gnawing his feet) or attitude (when Fearless Franny cowers behind your skirts or Iron Mike lets the tug toy fall from his mouth) can be more significant than physiological changes. The thing to remember is this: Dogs don't suddenly change their habits or their minds. The cause may be physical, emotional, or environmental, but you can't know which until you investigate. Always bring changes in behavior that last longer than a day or two to the attention of your veterinarian.

Home Checkups

Routinely checking out your Yorkie's physical condition is no big deal. It happens naturally during the grooming process—all the more reason for treasuring that time together. All abnormal findings mean a prompt visit to the veterinarian, as these conditions can become much more difficult to treat if neglected. In most cases you will be given medications and other treatments to administer at home.

Eyes

Some secretions are normal. Problems can be prevented with a few simple practices: keep hair out of the eyes, clean accumulated brownish matter from the corners of your Yorkie's eyes daily, don't cut hair beneath the eyes because short ends may then stick into the eyes, and don't let your Yorkie ride with her head outside the car.

Watch for these signs of abnormality in the eyes: thick, stringy discharge; yellow or white discharge; excessive tearing; excessive dryness; redness; squinting.

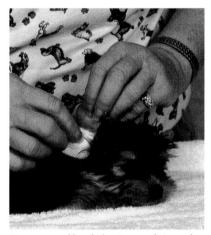

Ears

Yorkie ears are pinkish inside, with a dry and slightly waxy feel. A few wisps of hair may be visible in the ear canal. Prevent problems by keeping ears dry; clean only with cotton swabs moistened with mineral oil.

Prevent ear problems by keeping your dog's ears dry and clean. Clean only the parts of the ear you can see, and never stick anything into your dog's ear canal.

Watch for these signs of abnormality in the ears: discharge or any accumulated debris, large amounts or a wad of hair inside the ear, redness, swollen appearance, odor, areas that are warm and sensitive to the touch.

Teeth

The Yorkie's top and bottom teeth should meet and be clean, and each tooth should have its own space in the jaw. Prevent problems by starting during puppyhood to clean your Yorkie's teeth with a bit of gauze or a thin washcloth wrapped around your finger. Dip the cloth in a paste of baking soda and water.

Watch for these signs of abnormality in the mouth: teeth crowded together and overlapping, double teeth (usually the canines—the pointy "fangs"), tan or brown matter on the teeth, bad odor, swollen or red gums.

Skin and Coat

The skin should be clean and supple, the brushed coat should be lustrous. Yorkie coats come in three textures: silky, cottony, and woolly. The silky coat

Overall, your dog should look lean, muscular, and firm.

feels cool and has a metallic sheen; cottony and woolly coats have a warm feel, and even though they cannot gleam like a silky coat, they still can have a healthy luster. To prevent skin and coat problems, make sure your Yorkie has a good diet, lots of exercise, no worms or other parasites, and lives in a happy, loving home. Also, keep the heat in your home at a moderate level, and use a humidifier to add moisture to the air in the winter.

Watch for these signs of abnormality in the skin and coat: brittle or broken hair; thinning or bare patches; dry or oily scales; a dull, lifeless coat; bad odor; or cysts, scabs, or other growths on the skin.

Anal and Genital Regions

The anal and genital regions of your Yorkie, especially if the dog has been spayed or neutered, should not preoccupy the dog, except for proper cleaning after eliminating. To prevent problems, spay or neuter your dog and have your veterinarian promptly investigate any excessive licking or fussing with this area.

If the anal sacs (two small glands near the anus) have become clogged with glandular secretions that are normally released during bowel movements, the contents will have to be manually expressed by your dog's veterinarian. If more fiber in the diet and increased exercise don't prevent the problem from recurring, your veterinarian may teach you how to empty the glands yourself.

Watch for these signs of abnormality in the anal and genital regions: inflammation or discharge from the penis or vagina, odor, swollen or reddened area around the anus, scooting (when a dog drags her rear along the ground).

Overall Appearance

Your Yorkie should be a lean, firm, muscular package. (You wish you had a body like that!) Her limbs should be straight, her back level, her head held high, and her tail should wag a lot. To prevent problems in overall conditioning, make sure your Yorkie is allowed to live the active, vigorous life of a dog, not a toy.

Watch for these signs of abnormality in overall appearance: poor muscle tone; too little or too much weight; lack of energy, vitality, or interest.

Health Problems: Signs and Symptoms

Symptoms are not diseases. They are signs that something is wrong, and they should never be ignored. The "something" may be minor, or it may be major. If you're not sure, it is always better to be too cautious and take your Yorkie to the veterinarian right away. It's such a relief to be told, "It's nothing serious" that you

A sleepy dog is not necessarily sick, but prolonged lethargy can be a sign of a problem.

won't even mind the time and money spent. On the other hand, delaying too long and then being told, "If we'd only seen her sooner . . ." can haunt you forever. Here are some common signs that something is wrong.

Constipation

If your Yorkie strains repeatedly without passing stool, she is constipated. Not having a bowel movement one day is not constipation. If your Yorkie has a long coat, make sure that hair and stool have not become matted together, causing an external blockage.

Simple constipation in dogs is usually the result of not enough fiber in the diet, not enough fat, or not enough exercise. Eating bones or indigestible matter, such as grass, can also cause constipation. Try giving your Yorkie about a half teaspoon of mineral oil mixed in with her food. If that doesn't work within a few hours, make an appointment to visit your veterinarian.

Coughing

Coughing can have a variety of causes, virtually all of which need professional treatment. Many Yorkies and other toy dogs suffer from collapsing trachea, which causes irritation and coughing. The condition is permanent and progressive, but your veterinarian can advise you on different treatment options. Two things you can do are make sure your Yorkie is not overweight and avoid putting any pressure on the windpipe (another reason I like to see a Yorkie in a harness rather than on a leash).

Diarrhea

Frequent, loose, or watery stools can also be caused by many different things. One or two loose bowel movements may be the result of a minor upset; six or more should probably be taken seriously, as dehydration can result. Another factor that will help you decide how quickly you take your Yorkie to the vet is whether she's acting sick or has a fever. Uncomplicated diarrhea can be treated for a day by withholding all food for twelve hours, then feeding very bland food such as cooked chicken, soft-boiled eggs, or macaroni and giving about a teaspoon of Kaopectate every six hours. If there's blood or mucous in the diarrhea, vomiting, fever, or generalized sickness, take the dog to the veterinarian.

Frequent Urination

Frequent and urgent urination of scant amounts usually signals a bladder infection. If you see this sign, try to get a urine sample to take to your veterinarian

Puppies do get into everything, and diarrhea or vomiting can be the result.

for testing. To do this, wait until your Yorkie either squats or lifts a leg, then slide a saucer underneath to catch the urine. You may or may not see blood in the sample.

Limping

By careful observation, you should be able to tell which limb is hurting and, sometimes, why. Holding a foot up usually means there's something stuck on or between the pads. If the dog has just jumped or fallen from some height, the cause is obvious, although the severity of the injury may not be.

Pacing/Panting

Mostly, pacing and panting is a sign of anxiety, although it can also accompany pain. Examine your Yorkie carefully and gently to see if you can find something that hurts. The Wee once went into a state of feverish pacing and panting, and when I put my hands on her, I was horrified to find that her abdomen was hugely distended and tight as a drum. Certain that she had bloat, a gravely serious condition that results when the stomach twists and traps gas inside, I rushed her to the Animal Medical Center in New York City. (I had never heard of a toy dog having bloat, but I wasn't taking any chances.) On the ride in the car, I discovered that she had gas all right, but it definitely was able to escape! When it did, her anxiety escaped with it, and within minutes she was completely back to normal. I still had the emergency staff check her out though.

Pawing at the Mouth

Assuming the dog is not choking (unable to breathe), this sign invariably means there is something stuck in the mouth. Open the mouth gently if you can; if you can see the whole object, you may be able to remove it yourself. Use extreme caution in removing anything that has penetrated the skin, as it's very difficult to hold a Yorkie's head completely still. Even if you can remove the object, it may need to be followed up by an antibiotic.

Rubbing at the Eye

Dogs rub both eyes persistently against the sofa or carpet when their eyes are generally itchy or irritated due to such things as smoke or allergies. But when they rub one eye frantically or paw at it, they are in pain. Either there is something in that eye, or there is a scratch on the cornea. I consider this an emergency, as dogs can do a lot of damage to themselves until they get relief. Chances are they will not tolerate your looking around to see what the problem is.

Any matter or runniness at the eyes or nose should be checked out by a vet.

Scratching

Dogs scratch from fleas, mites, and other things that bite; from dry skin; from shampoo residue; and from allergies of many kinds. If your Yorkie is scratching a particular body part, such as her ear, look there for the problem. Some dogs are very allergic to fleas, and even if the fleas (or single flea) are removed, the scratching goes on . . . and on. If a flea bath or regular shampoo followed by thorough rinsing doesn't seem to help, you'll need your veterinarian to investigate. Itchy skin is another condition that is thought to be exacerbated by an unwholesome lifestyle, overprocessed foods, overmedication, injudicious use of pesticides, and so on.

Shivering

Shivering and trembling can look similar, but the circumstances, as well as the dog's expression and body language, can usually distinguish the two. A cold dog looks miserable, is usually wet, and is probably trying to climb up your pant leg. A shivering dog who has other symptoms of illness, such as staggering or confusion, or who has just suffered some sort of trauma, needs emergency treatment. A trembling dog looks and acts fearful, with a tucked, cowering posture. This behavior is most often displayed in the veterinarian's office, so there's no need to take her there for evaluation! If you don't know why your Yorkie is trembling and there's any possibility that she might have ingested poison, this is obviously an emergency situation.

Body temperature is a big issue for little dogs. You may have to take special steps to keep your dog comfortable.

Vomiting

Dogs vomit for many reasons, mostly dietary ones. Vomiting once or twice, without other signs of sickness or distress, can be treated at home. Withhold food and water for twelve hours, then offer very small meals of bland food and, if that stays down, repeat in four hours. Offer only minute amounts of water. If all goes well for twenty-four hours, feed normal portions of bland food for one more day just to be on the safe side. Frequent vomiting, unproductive retching, or vomiting with blood, pain, fever, or diarrhea needs prompt veterinary attention.

Internal Parasites

Roundworms

Roundworms, probably the most common of the internal parasites, show up most frequently in puppies, although it is possible for adult dogs and even people to be infested. Dogs often pick them up by sniffing feces left behind by

Your dog can pick up a variety of common internal parasites from infected garden soil.

infected dogs. Because of the easy transmission of this parasite, it is always a good idea to make sure feces left behind by both your dog and other dogs are picked up every day.

When treated early, roundworms should not turn into a serious health concern. However, a heavy infestation can severely affect your dog's health. The adult female roundworm can lay up to 200,000 eggs a day, which are then passed out with the dog's feces. Mature roundworms, which will also be passed during bowel movements, resemble strands of spaghetti and can be eight to ten inches long. A puppy with an infestation of this type will usually have a pot belly, a thin appearance, and a coat lacking shine and luster. The dog may also show signs of infestation in other ways: vomiting, sometimes bringing up worms, diarrhea, weight loss, and an overall unhealthy look. Young puppies already infested at birth can die within two to three weeks, as severe dehydration will often accompany these symptoms.

Roundworms can be more dangerous in humans, so it is especially important to make sure your own surroundings are kept clean of animal waste and that you contact your veterinarian as soon as you suspect your dog may have the parasite.

Hookworms

Hookworms are reason for somewhat more alarm than roundworms. These bloodsucking parasites can cause anemia in both puppies and adults, and their eggs are also passed through feces. These very hardy eggs can survive for long periods of time in sand or soil, even after the feces have been removed. Puppies are often infected through their mother's milk, but hookworms can also enter the dog through the feet and the skin. The parasite burrows through the skin and migrates to the intestinal tract, where it attaches to the intestinal wall. Hookworms can also be acquired by humans through similar means, often through the skin of bare feet. It is therefore important to be cautious when walking barefoot in sandy or earthy areas where dogs are likely to defecate.

A dog infected with hookworms will usually pass a somewhat slimy stool or have bloody diarrhea. Other symptoms may include weakness, pale gums, weight loss, and dehydration. Take your dog to the veterinarian immediately if you suspect she may have been infected with hookworms; bring along a stool sample for analysis.

Tapeworms

Diligent flea control is necessary to reduce the chances of tapeworm infection in your Yorkie. These are the second most common parasite in dogs and are usually acquired when the dog swallows a flea while chewing at herself to scratch a flea bite. The flea serves as an intermediate host for the parasite. After gaining access to the dog's system, the tapeworm will attach to the wall of the intestines and support itself by absorbing nutrients.

You will most likely notice that your dog has tapeworms when you see rice-like segments in the dog's stool, in the fur around the dog's anus, and perhaps even on her bedding. Tapeworms are certainly not the most devastating of internal parasites, but they still warrant prompt veterinary attention. Usually one deworming will rid the dog of the infestation, but the next round of fleas will likely present the same problem. Keeping fleas under control is the only way to effectively rid your Yorkie of tapeworms completely.

Whipworms

Whipworms, which feed on blood, live in the large intestine. These threadlike parasites are somewhat thicker at one end than at the other and reach two to three inches in length at maturity. Their eggs are passed in feces, and once left behind in the soil, the eggs can survive for many years. An infected dog has usually picked up the parasite by digging and sniffing in infected soil, which can also be the source of infection for humans. Since the eggs can survive for such a long time, disinfecting your environment can be difficult. The most effective precautionary measures include cleaning dog runs and areas where dogs frequently defecate with a bleach-and-water mixture, wearing gloves when digging in soil likely to be infected, and being cautious about where you choose to walk barefoot, whether in the park, at the beach, or even in your own yard.

Diagnosing a case of whipworms can be difficult since the worms do not release eggs into the stool every day. If you suspect that your dog may be infected, collect stool samples for several days in a row and take them to your veterinarian for analysis. Suspect infestation if your dog has diarrhea, often bloody or watery, and if she has a thin, anemic look with a poor coat. Severe bowel problems and anemia usually result from these parasites, so take your Yorkie to your veterinarian as soon as you notice symptoms of this sort.

Heartworms

Dogs become infected by heartworms when they are bitten by a mosquito that carries the parasite. Adult heartworms live in the heart and lungs of an infected

Talk to your veterinarian about a heartworm prevention program that is right for your climate and area of the country.

dog, and their offspring (microfilaria) circulate in the bloodstream. The likelihood that your dog will become infected depends somewhat on the climate in which you live. Areas that tend to be warm and moist for most of the year will see an increased population of mosquitoes and will therefore see an increased number of heartworm infections. Your veterinarian should be able to advise you on the risk in your particular area.

There are pills that you can give your dog to prevent heartworm infection, but it's important to first make sure that your dog isn't already infested. If she is, giving the treatment will only worsen her condition and may result in death. Always consult with your veterinarian before beginning any preventive care of this nature.

The adult heartworm can cause severe illness and even death due to congestive heart failure and/or blood clots in the lungs. Suspect heartworms if you and your veterinarian see signs of liver problems, coughing, and weight loss. Heartworm infestation is easily confirmed by a blood test.

Coccidia

As unpleasant as the idea may be, dogs may sometimes eat their own feces or the feces of other dogs. If those feces are contaminated with this protozoan, the dog will become infected. (A protozoan is a one-celled animal that finds its way into a dog's system as a tiny cyst ingested with contaminated feces. These cysts eventually wind up in the lining of the bowel, where they mature.) Dogs affected by coccidia are most often puppies, who have been infected by their mothers before birth. It is possible for adult dogs to have it or to be carriers. Dogs can reinfect themselves by touching their own feces or that of other infected dogs, so good sanitation is the key to keeping your dog free of coccidia.

One of the first symptoms you are likely to see is a mucuslike diarrhea, sometimes containing blood. Other symptoms include runny eyes and nose, cough, dehydration, anemia, weight loss, and weakness.

Giardia

Giardia is a protozoan that is common in wild animals and is often spread to domestic animals and people through contaminated drinking water. Your Yorkie may come down with a case of giardia if she's gone exploring through the woods or other areas inhabited by wild animals or has been drinking water from contaminated puddles. Diarrhea and bloody stools after a hiking or camping outing are usually the best indicators of an infection of this sort.

How to Make a Canine First-Aid Kit

If your dog hurts herself, even a minor cut, it can be very upsetting for both of you. Having a first-aid kit handy will help you to help her, calmly and efficiently. What should be in your canine first-aid kit?

- Antibiotic ointment
- Antiseptic and antibacterial cleansing wipes
- Benadryl
- Cotton-tipped applicators
- Disposable razor
- Elastic wrap bandages
- Extra leash and collar
- First-aid tape of various widths
- Gauze bandage roll
- Gauze pads of different sizes, including eye pads
- Hydrogen peroxide
- Instant cold compress
- Kaopectate tablets or liquid
- Latex gloves
- Lubricating jelly
- Muzzle
- Nail clippers
- Pen, pencil, and paper for notes and directions
- Pepto-Bismol
- Round-ended scissors and pointy scissors
- Safety pins
- Sterile saline eyewash
- Thermometer (rectal)
- Tweezers

First Aid

The following are the steps for performing artificial respiration and CPR. These procedures should be performed as you're on your way to a veterinary or emergency clinic in a life-threatening situation. Do not practice artificial respiration on a dog who is breathing. Do not practice CPR on a dog who is breathing or who has a pulse.

Artificial Respiration

1. Lay the Yorkie on her right side on a flat, hard surface.
2. Open the mouth, extend the neck, and pull the tongue forward, then close the mouth again and hold it shut.
3. Position your head so you can see the Yorkie's chest, then put your mouth around her nose and blow in for about three seconds. Do not blow with a

Knowing canine first aid could save your dog's life.

lot of force; as long as you can see the chest expand, you are blowing hard enough.
4. Release and watch the chest fall.
5. Repeat until the dog breathes on her own or until you can turn her over to the veterinarian.

CPR

1. Lay the Yorkie on her right side on a flat, hard surface. If there are two people present and you can manage not to get in each other's way, have one perform artificial respiration and one massage the heart. If you are alone, you must do both, in alternating sets: one breath, six heart compressions, and repeat.
2. To compress the heart, grasp the Yorkie's chest with your thumb on one side of the sternum (the breastbone) and your fingers on the other, just behind the elbow. Obviously you can't reach the heart directly, so in order to "massage" it, you have to squeeze it between the ribs and the breastbone.
3. Squeeze firmly at the rate of one compression a second.
4. Continue until the heart beats on its own or until you are at the emergency clinic.

Senior Care

Toy dogs generally live longer than larger ones and seem to be in their prime at 7, 8, and 9 years of age, when larger breeds are already slowing down. Yorkies routinely live to be 13 or 14, and frequently even longer. So assuming all is well

When to Call the Veterinarian

Go to the vet right away or take your dog to an emergency veterinary clinic if:
- Your dog is choking
- Your dog is having trouble breathing
- Your dog has been injured and you cannot stop the bleeding within a few minutes
- Your dog has been stung or bitten by an insect and the site is swelling
- Your dog has been bitten by a snake
- Your dog has been bitten by another animal (including a dog) and shows any swelling or bleeding
- Your dog has touched, licked, or in any way been exposed to a poison
- Your dog has been burned by either heat or caustic chemicals
- Your dog has been hit by a car
- Your dog has any obvious broken bones or cannot put any weight on one of her limbs
- Your dog has a seizure

Make an appointment to see the vet as soon as possible if:
- Your dog has been bitten by a cat, another dog, or a wild animal
- Your dog has been injured and is still limping an hour later

with your Yorkie, the eighth, ninth, and tenth years are a good time to start thinking about and planning for the changes that will gradually come.

Eyes, Ears, and Activity

Signs of aging include failing eyesight and hearing, as well as greater sensitivity to temperature extremes. Your Yorkie may seem less eager to go outdoors and fling herself at the world. If so, it is more likely due to diminished sight or hearing than to arthritis or other joint problems that are common in large dogs of the same age.

When The Wee was around 12, she began to hang back on some of her outings. It was only when I realized that her reluctance was limited to her late-night walk that it dawned on me she might not be able to see after dark. Sure enough, she was more than happy to be active at that hour as long as we stayed in

- Your dog has unexplained swelling or redness
- Your dog's appetite changes
- Your dog vomits repeatedly and can't seem to keep food down, or drools excessively while eating
- You see any changes in your dog's urination or defecation (pain during elimination, change in regular habits, blood in urine or stool, diarrhea, foul-smelling stool)
- Your dog scoots her rear end on the floor
- Your dog's energy level, attitude, or behavior changes for no apparent reason
- Your dog has crusty or cloudy eyes, or excessive tearing or discharge
- Your dog's nose is dry or chapped, hot, crusty, or runny
- Your dog's ears smell foul, have a dark discharge, or seem excessively waxy
- Your dog's gums are inflamed or bleeding, her teeth look brown, or her breath is foul
- Your dog's skin is red, flaky, itchy, or inflamed, or she keeps chewing at certain spots
- Your dog's coat is dull, dry, brittle, or bare in spots
- Your dog's paws are red, swollen, tender, cracked, or the nails are split or too long
- Your dog is panting excessively, wheezing, unable to catch her breath, breathing heavily, or sounds strange when she breathes

brightly lit areas. So unless you have reason to think your Yorkie has stiff or painful joints, I would look for creative ways to keep her as physically active as she is able to be.

Routines and Rituals

For the most part, your aging Yorkie will appreciate a minimum of change and upset in her life. If you have any choice in the matter, this is not the time to relocate, to go back to work full time, or to add a new puppy—or person—to the household.

Feeding, walking, grooming, and other schedules are also best left the same, though by all means, make any modifications that are appropriate. For instance, most Yorkies will appreciate less grooming and bathing. If you haven't already

Dogs cherish their routines. As they age, change upsets them even more.

begun cutting the coat short, maybe it's time. The Wee never liked having her topknot tied up, so when she was middle-aged, I gave in and kept the hair on top of her head cut short.

Keeping Up with Grooming

Now more than ever, it's important to keep up with regular brushing and combing because your older Yorkie really will not like a marathon session to get out mats. Incidentally, deciding to have your dog's whole coat clipped off with an electric clipper is not the simple remedy it sounds. Yorkies who are not accustomed to the noise and vibration of the clippers can be quite unhappy about it, and shaving off a badly matted coat is a long, arduous process with considerable risk of "clipper burn" to sensitive senior skin.

Caring for Teeth

Ongoing care of the teeth is also important. Many Yorkies have had many or most of their teeth removed by the time they reach senior status. It's important to remember that teeth are not ornamental; a dog with many missing teeth is limited in the kinds of foods she can eat and is denied the birthright of all dogs—to chew.

No teeth, however, is better than rotten teeth. The bacteria that accompany dental disease can cause systemic infection and put extra strain on organs such as the kidneys, liver, and heart. In addition, loose teeth and sore, swollen gums are not only painful, but the terrible odor is bound to cause you to keep your Yorkie at arm's length—just when she deserves more than ever to be held close and cherished.

Making Allowances

Finally, as your Yorkie approaches the last lap of life, she may need a little extra help and consideration. Old dogs, like old humans, can get confused and forgetful sometimes and should never be scolded for lapses in housetraining. And as Senior Lamb Chop begins to spend more and more time sleeping, her preferred bed—even if it's yours—needs to be accessible.

For many years, The Wee was impressive at jumping into (our) bed. She would approach at a run, launch herself through the air from an improbable distance, land with her rear feet on the ledge where the mattress met the box spring, then give an additional little kick that took her over the top. She did this a dozen times a day, usually bringing along a juicy chew stick, a favorite toy, or a biscuit to bury in the pillows. The day came, however, when she was no longer able to get up on the bed. Being a dog, incapable of self-pity or regret, she wandered off to one of her other favorite spots. But Bill wasn't having any of that. In no time at all, he'd built a ramp up to the bed, complete with carpeting so she wouldn't slip. It took her two or three minutes to learn how to race up and down the ramp, and she did so for an additional two years, even after she'd become almost completely blind. Of course, it was our pleasure to accommodate The Wee in her old age, trying to repay in small human ways the incalculable joy she'd brought into our lives.

Part III

Enjoying Your Yorkie

Chapter 9

Training Your Yorkie

by Peggy Moran

Training makes your best friend better! A properly trained dog has a happier life and a longer life expectancy. He is also more appreciated by the people he encounters each day, both at home and out and about.

A trained dog walks nicely and joins his family often, going places untrained dogs cannot go. He is never rude or unruly, and he always happily comes when called. When he meets people for the first time, he greets them by sitting and waiting to be petted, rather than jumping up. At home he doesn't compete with his human family, and alone he is not destructive or overly anxious. He isn't continually nagged with words like "no," since he has learned not to misbehave in the first place. He is never shamed, harshly punished, or treated unkindly, and he is a well-loved, involved member of the family.

Sounds good, doesn't it? If you are willing to invest some time, thought, and patience, the words above could soon be used to describe your dog (though perhaps changing "he" to "she"). Educating your pet in a positive way is fun and easy, and there is no better gift you can give your pet than the guarantee of improved understanding and a great relationship.

This chapter will explain how to offer kind leadership, reshape your pet's behavior in a positive and practical way, and even get a head start on simple obedience training.

Understanding Builds the Bond

Dog training is a learning adventure on both ends of the leash. Before attempting to teach their dog new behaviors or change unwanted ones, thoughtful dog owners take the time to understand why their pets behave the way they do, and how their own behavior can be either a positive or negative influence on their dog.

Canine Nature

Loving dogs as much as we do, it's easy to forget they are a completely different species. Despite sharing our homes and living as appreciated members of our families, dogs do not think or learn exactly the same way people do. Even if you love your dog like a child, you must remember to respect the fact that he is actually a dog.

Dogs have no idea when their behavior is inappropriate from a human perspective. They are not aware of the value of possessions they chew or of messes they make or the worry they sometimes seem to cause. While people tend to look at behavior as good and bad or right and wrong, dogs just discover what works and what doesn't work. Then they behave accordingly, learning from their own experiences and increasing or reducing behaviors to improve results for themselves.

You might wonder, "But don't dogs want to please us"? My answer is yes, provided your pleasure reflects back to them in positive ways they can feel and appreciate. Dogs do things for *dog* reasons, and everything they do works for them in some way or they wouldn't be doing it!

The Social Dog

Our pets descended from animals who lived in tightly knit, cooperative social groups. Though far removed in appearance and lifestyle from their ancestors, our dogs still relate in many of the same ways their wild relatives did. And in their relationships with one another, wild canids either lead or follow.

Canine ranking relationships are not about cruelty and power; they are about achievement and abilities. Competent dogs with high levels of drive and confidence step up, while deferring dogs step aside. But followers don't get the short end of the stick; they benefit from the security of having a more competent dog at the helm.

Our domestic dogs still measure themselves against other members of their group—us! Dog owners whose actions lead to positive results have willing, secure followers. But dogs may step up and fill the void or cut loose and do their own thing when their people fail to show capable leadership. When dogs are pushy, aggressive, and rude, or independent and unwilling, it's not because they have designs on the role of "master." It is more likely their owners failed to provide consistent leadership.

Dogs in training benefit from their handler's good leadership. Their education flows smoothly because they are impressed. Being in charge doesn't require you to physically dominate or punish your dog. You simply need to make some subtle changes in the way you relate to him every day.

Lead Your Pack!

Create schedules and structure daily activities. Dogs are creatures of habit and routines will create security. Feed meals at the same times each day and also try to schedule regular walks, training practices, and toilet outings. Your predictability will help your dog be patient.

Ask your dog to perform a task. Before releasing him to food or freedom, have him do something as simple as sit on command. Teach him that cooperation earns great results!

Give a release prompt (such as "let's go") when going through doors leading outside. This is a better idea than allowing your impatient pup to rush past you.

Pet your dog when he is calm, not when he is excited. Turn your touch into a tool that relaxes and settles.

Reward desirable rather than inappropriate behavior. Petting a jumping dog (who hasn't been invited up) reinforces jumping. Pet sitting dogs, and only invite lap dogs up after they've first "asked" by waiting for your invitation.

Replace personal punishment with positive reinforcement. Show a dog what *to do,* and motivate him to want to do it, and there will be no need to punish him for what he should *not do.* Dogs naturally follow, without the need for force or harshness.

Play creatively and appropriately. Your dog will learn the most about his social rank when he is playing with you. During play, dogs work to control toys and try to get the best of one another in a friendly way. The wrong sorts of play can create problems: For example, tug of war can lead to aggressiveness. Allowing your dog to control toys during play may result in possessive guarding when he has something he really values, such as a bone. Dogs who are chased during play may later run away from you when you approach to leash them. The right kinds of play will help increase your dog's social confidence while you gently assert your leadership.

How Dogs Learn (and How They Don't)

Dog training begins as a meeting of minds—yours and your dog's. Though the end goal may be to get your dog's body to behave in a specific way, training starts as a mind game. Your dog is learning all the time by observing the consequences of his actions and social interactions. He is always seeking out what he perceives as desirable and trying to avoid what he perceives as undesirable.

He will naturally repeat a behavior that either brings him more good stuff or makes bad stuff go away (these are both types of reinforcement). He will naturally avoid a behavior that brings him more bad stuff or makes the good stuff go away (these are both types of punishment).

Both reinforcement and punishment can be perceived as either the direct result of something the dog did himself, or as coming from an outside source.

Using Life's Rewards

Your best friend is smart and he is also cooperative. When the best things in life can only be had by working with you, your dog will view you as a facilitator. You unlock doors to all of the positively reinforcing experiences he values: his freedom, his friends at the park, food, affection, walks, and play. The trained dog accompanies you through those doors and waits to see what working with you will bring.

Rewarding your dog for good behavior is called positive reinforcement, and, as we've just seen, it increases the likelihood that he will repeat that behavior. The perfect reward is anything your dog wants that is safe and appropriate. Don't limit yourself to toys, treats, and things that come directly from you. Harness life's positives—barking at squirrels, chasing a falling leaf, bounding away from you at the dog park, pausing for a moment to sniff everything—and allow your dog to earn access to those things as rewards that come from cooperating with you. When he looks at you, when he sits, when he comes when you call—any prompted behavior can earn one of life's rewards. When he works with you, he earns the things he most appreciates; but when he tries to get those things on his own, he cannot. Rather than seeing you as someone who always says "no," your dog will view you as the one who says "let's go!" He will *want* to follow.

What About Punishment?

Not only is it unnecessary to personally punish dogs, it is abusive. No matter how convinced you are that your dog "knows right from wrong," in reality he will associate personal punishment with the punisher. The resulting cowering, "guilty"-looking postures are actually displays of submission and fear. Later,

Purely Positive Reinforcement

With positive training, we emphasize teaching dogs what they should do to earn reinforcements, rather than punishing them for unwanted behaviors.

- Focus on teaching "do" rather than "don't." For example, a sitting dog isn't jumping.
- Use positive reinforcers that are valuable to your dog and the situation: A tired dog values rest; a confined dog values freedom.
- Play (appropriately)!
- Be a consistent leader.
- Set your dog up for success by anticipating and preventing problems.
- Notice and reward desirable behavior, and give him lots of attention when he is being good.
- Train ethically. Use humane methods and equipment that do not frighten or hurt your dog.
- When you are angry, walk away and plan a positive strategy.
- Keep practice sessions short and sweet. Five to ten minutes, three to five times a day is best.

when the punisher isn't around and the coast is clear, the same behavior he was punished for—such as raiding a trash can—might bring a self-delivered, very tasty result. The punished dog hasn't learned not to misbehave; he has learned to not get caught.

Does punishment ever have a place in dog training? Many people will heartily insist it does not. But dog owners often get frustrated as they try to stick to the path of all-positive reinforcement. It sure sounds great, but is it realistic, or even natural, to *never* say "no" to your dog?

A wild dog's life is not *all* positive. Hunger and thirst are both examples of negative reinforcement; the resulting discomfort motivates the wild dog to seek food and water. He encounters natural aversives such as pesky insects; mats in his coat; cold days; rainy days; sweltering hot days; and occasional run-ins with thorns, brambles, skunks, bees, and other nastiness. These all affect his behavior, as he tries to avoid the bad stuff whenever possible. The wild dog also occasionally encounters social punishers from others in his group when he gets too pushy. Starting with a growl or a snap from Mom, and later some mild and ritualized discipline from other members of his four-legged family, he learns to modify behaviors that elicit grouchy responses.

Our pet dogs don't naturally experience all positive results either, because they learn from their surroundings and from social experiences with other dogs. Watch a group of pet dogs playing together and you'll see a very old educational system still being used. As they wrestle and attempt to assert themselves, you'll notice many mouth-on-neck moments. Their playful biting is inhibited, with no intention to cause harm, but their message is clear: "Say uncle or this could hurt more!"

Observing that punishment does occur in nature, some people may feel compelled to try to be like the big wolf with their pet dogs. Becoming aggressive or heavy-handed with your pet will backfire! Your dog will not be impressed, nor will he want to follow you. Punishment causes dogs to change their behavior to avoid or escape discomfort and threats. Threatened dogs will either become very passive and offer submissive, appeasing postures, attempt to flee, or rise to the occasion and fight back. When people personally punish their dogs in an angry manner, one of these three defensive mechanisms will be triggered. Which one depends on a dog's genetic temperament as well as his past social experiences. Since we don't want to make our pets feel the need to avoid or escape us, personal punishment has no place in our training.

Remote Consequences

Sometimes, however, all-positive reinforcement is just not enough. That's because not all reinforcement comes from us. An inappropriate behavior can be self-reinforcing—just doing it makes the dog feel better in some way, whether you are there to say "good boy!" or not. Some examples are eating garbage, pulling the stuffing out of your sofa, barking at passersby, or urinating on the floor.

Although you don't want to personally punish your dog, the occasional deterrent may be called for to help derail these kinds of self-rewarding misbehaviors. In these cases, mild forms of impersonal or remote punishment can be used as part of a correction. The goal isn't to make your dog feel bad or to "know he has done wrong," but to help redirect him to alternate behaviors that are more acceptable to you.

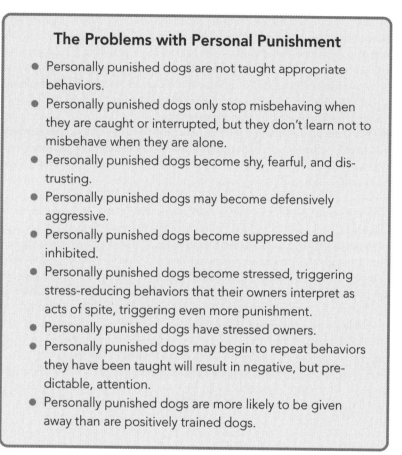

The Problems with Personal Punishment

- Personally punished dogs are not taught appropriate behaviors.
- Personally punished dogs only stop misbehaving when they are caught or interrupted, but they don't learn not to misbehave when they are alone.
- Personally punished dogs become shy, fearful, and distrusting.
- Personally punished dogs may become defensively aggressive.
- Personally punished dogs become suppressed and inhibited.
- Personally punished dogs become stressed, triggering stress-reducing behaviors that their owners interpret as acts of spite, triggering even more punishment.
- Personally punished dogs have stressed owners.
- Personally punished dogs may begin to repeat behaviors they have been taught will result in negative, but predictable, attention.
- Personally punished dogs are more likely to be given away than are positively trained dogs.

You do this by pairing a slightly startling, totally impersonal sound with an equally impersonal and *very mild* remote consequence. The impersonal sound might be a single shake of an empty plastic pop bottle with pennies in it, held out of your dog's sight. Or you could use a vocal expression such as "eh!" delivered with you looking *away* from your misbehaving dog.

Pair your chosen sound—the penny bottle or "eh!"—with either a slight tug on his collar or a sneaky spritz on the rump from a water bottle. Do this right *as* he touches something he should not; bad timing will confuse your dog and undermine your training success.

To keep things under your control and make sure you get the timing right, it's best to do this as a setup. "Accidentally" drop a shoe on the floor, and then help your dog learn some things are best avoided. As he sniffs the shoe say "eh!" without looking at him and give a *slight* tug against his collar. This sound will quickly become meaningful as a correction all by itself—sometimes after just one setup—making the tug correction obsolete. The tug lets your dog see that you were right; going for that shoe *was* a bad idea! Your wise dog will be more likely to heed your warning next time, and probably move closer to you where it's safe. Be a good friend and pick up the nasty shoe. He'll be relieved and you'll look heroic. Later, when he's home alone and encounters a stray shoe, he'll want to give it a wide berth.

Your negative marking sound will come in handy in the future, when your dog begins to venture down the wrong behavioral path. The goal is not to announce your disapproval or to threaten your dog. You are not telling him to stop or showing how *you* feel about his behavior. You are sounding a warning to a friend who's venturing off toward danger—"I wouldn't if I were you!" Suddenly, there is an abrupt, rather startling, noise! Now is the moment to redirect him and help him earn positive reinforcement. That interrupted behavior will become something he wants to avoid in the future, but he won't want to avoid you.

Practical Commands for Family Pets

Before you begin training your dog, let's look at some equipment you'll want to have on hand:

- **A buckle collar** is fine for most dogs. If your dog pulls *very* hard, try a head collar, a device similar to a horse halter that helps reduce pulling by turning the dog's head. *Do not* use a choke chain (sometimes called a training collar), because they cause physical harm even when used correctly.
- **Six-foot training leash and twenty-six–foot retractable leash.**
- **A few empty plastic soda bottles with about twenty pennies in each one.** This will be used to impersonally interrupt misbehaviors before redirecting dogs to more positive activities.
- **A favorite squeaky toy,** to motivate, attract attention, and reward your dog during training.

Lure your dog to take just a few steps with you on the leash by being inviting and enthusiastic. Make sure you reward him for his efforts.

Baby Steps

Allow your young pup to drag a short, lightweight leash attached to a buckle collar for a few *supervised* moments, several times each day. At first the leash may annoy him and he may jump around a bit trying to get away from it. Distract him with your squeaky toy or a bit of his kibble and he'll quickly get used to his new "tail."

Begin walking him on the leash by holding the end and following him. As he adapts, you can begin to assert gentle direct pressure to teach him to follow you. Don't jerk or yank, or he will become afraid to walk when the leash is on. If he becomes hesitant, squat down facing him and let him figure out that by moving toward you he is safe and secure. If he remains confused or frightened and doesn't come to you, go to him and help him understand that you provide safe harbor while he's on the leash. Then back away a few steps and try again to lure him to you. As he learns that you are the "home base," he'll want to follow when you walk a few steps, waiting for you to stop, squat down, and make him feel great.

So Attached to You!

The next step in training your dog—and this is a very important one—is to begin spending at least an hour or more each day with him on a four- to six-foot leash, held by or tethered to you. This training will increase his attachment to you—literally!—as you sit quietly or walk about, tending to your household business. When you are quiet, he'll learn it is time to settle; when you are active, he'll learn to move with you. Tethering also keeps him out of trouble when you are busy but still want his company. It is a great alternative to confining a dog, and can be used instead of crating any time you're home and need to slow him down a bit.

Rotating your dog from supervised freedom to tethered time to some quiet time in the crate or his gated area gives him a diverse and balanced day while he is learning. Two confined or tethered hours is the most you should require of your dog in one stretch, before changing to some supervised freedom, play, or a walk.

The dog in training may, at times, be stressed by all of the changes he is dealing with. Provide a stress outlet, such as a toy to chew on, when he is confined or tethered. He will settle into his quiet time more quickly and completely. Always be sure to provide several rounds of daily play and free time (in a fenced area or on your retractable leash) in addition to plenty of chewing materials.

Tethering your dog is a great way to keep him calm and under control, but still with you.

Dog Talk

Dogs don't speak in words, but they do have a language—body language. They use postures, vocalizations, movements, facial gestures, odors, and touch—usually with their mouths—to communicate what they are feeling and thinking.

We also "speak" using body language. We have quite an array of postures, movements, and facial gestures that accompany our touch and language as we attempt to communicate with our pets. And our dogs can quickly figure us out!

Alone, without associations, words are just noises. But, because we pair them with meaningful body language, our dogs make the connection. Dogs can really learn to understand much of what we *say,* if what we *do* at the same time is consistent.

The Positive Marker

Start your dog's education with one of the best tricks in dog training: Pair various positive reinforcers—food, a toy, touch—with a sound such as a click on a clicker (which you can get at the pet supply store) or a spoken word like "good!" or "yes!" This will enable you to later "mark" your dog's desirable behaviors.

It seems too easy: Just say "yes!" and give the dog his toy. (Or use whatever sound and reward you have chosen.) Later, when you make your marking sound right at the instant your dog does the right thing, he will know you are going to be giving him something good for that particular action. And he'll be eager to repeat the behavior to hear you mark it again!

Next, you must teach your dog to understand the meaning of cues you'll be using to ask him to perform specific behaviors. This is easy, too. Does he already do things you might like him to do on command? Of course! He lies down, he sits, he picks things up, he drops them again, he comes to you. All of the behaviors you'd like to control are already part of your dog's natural repertoire. The trick is getting him to offer those behaviors when you ask for them. And that means you have to teach him to associate a particular behavior on his part with a particular behavior on your part.

Sit Happens

Teach your dog an important new rule: From now on, he is only touched and petted when he is either sitting or lying down. You won't need to ask him to sit; in fact, you should not. Just keeping him tethered near you so there isn't much to do but stand, be ignored, or settle, and wait until sit happens.

He may pester you a bit, but be stoic and unresponsive. Starting now, when *you* are sitting down, a sitting dog is the only one you see and pay attention to. He will eventually sit, and as he does, attach the word "sit"—but don't be too excited or he'll jump right back up. Now mark with your positive sound that promises something good, then reward him with a slow, quiet, settling pet.

Training requires consistent reinforcement. Ask others to also wait until your dog is sitting and calm to touch him, and he will associate being petted with being relaxed. Be sure you train your dog to associate everyone's touch with quiet bonding.

Reinforcing "Sit" as a Command

Since your dog now understands one concept of working for a living—sit to earn petting—you can begin to shape and reinforce his desire to sit. Hold toys, treats, his bowl of food, and turn into a statue. But don't prompt him to sit! Instead, remain frozen and unavailable, looking somewhere out into space, over his head. He will put on a bit of a show, trying to get a response from you, and may offer various behaviors, but only one will push your button—sitting. Wait for him to offer the "right" behavior, and when he does, you unfreeze. Say "sit," then mark with an excited "good!" and give him the toy or treat with a release command—"OK!"

When you notice spontaneous sits occurring, be sure to take advantage of those free opportunities to make your command sequence meaningful and positive. Say "sit" as you observe sit happen—then mark with "good!" and praise, pet, or reward the dog. Soon, every time you look at your dog he'll be sitting and looking right back at you!

Now, after thirty days of purely positive practice, it's time to give him a test. When he is just walking around doing his own thing, suddenly ask him to sit. He'll probably do it right away. If he doesn't, do *not* repeat your command, or you'll just undermine its meaning ("sit" means sit *now;* the command is not "sit, sit, sit, sit"). Instead, get something he likes and let him know you have it. Wait for him to offer the sit—he will—then say "sit!" and complete your marking and rewarding sequence.

OK

"OK" will probably rate as one of your dog's favorite words. It's like the word "recess" to schoolchildren. It is the word used to release your dog from a command. You can introduce "OK" during your "sit" practice. When he gets up from a sit, say "OK" to tell him the sitting is finished. Soon that sound will mean "freedom."

Make it even more meaningful and positive. Whenever he spontaneously bounds away, say "OK!" Squeak a toy, and when he notices and shows interest, toss it for him.

Down

I've mentioned that you should only pet your dog when he is either sitting or lying down. Now, using the approach I've just introduced for "sit," teach your dog to lie down. You will be a statue, and hold something he would like to get but that you'll only release to a dog who is lying down. It helps to lower the desired item to the floor in front of him, still not speaking and not letting him have it until he offers you the new behavior you are seeking.

Lower your dog's reward to the floor to help him figure out what behavior will earn him his reward.

He may offer a sit and then wait expectantly, but you must make him keep searching for the new trick that triggers your generosity. Allow your dog to experiment and find the right answer, even if he has to search around for it first. When he lands on "down" and learns it is another behavior that works, he'll offer it more quickly the next time.

Don't say "down" until he lies down, to tightly associate your prompt with the correct behavior. To say "down, down, down" as he is sitting, looking at you, or pawing at the toy would make "down" mean those behaviors instead! Whichever behavior he offers, a training opportunity has been created. Once you've attached and shaped both sitting and lying down, you can ask for both behaviors with your verbal prompts, "sit" or "down." Be sure to only reinforce the "correct" reply!

Stay

"Stay" can easily be taught as an extension of what you've already been practicing. To teach "stay," you follow the entire sequence for reinforcing a "sit" or "down," except you wait a bit longer before you give the release word, "OK!" Wait a second or two longer during each practice before saying "OK!" and releasing your dog to the positive reinforcer (toy, treat, or one of life's other rewards).

You can step on the leash to help your dog understand the down-stay, but only do this when he is already lying down. You don't want to hurt him!

If he gets up before you've said "OK," you have two choices: pretend the release was your idea and quickly interject "OK!" as he breaks; or, if he is more experienced and practiced, mark the behavior with your correction sound—"eh!"— and then gently put him back on the spot, wait for him to lie down, and begin again. Be sure the next three practices are a success. Ask him to wait for just a second, and release him before he can be wrong. You need to keep your dog feeling like more of a success than a failure as you begin to test his training in increasingly more distracting and difficult situations.

As he gets the hang of it—he stays until you say "OK"— you can gradually push for longer times—up to a minute on a sit-stay, and up to three minutes on a down-stay. You can also gradually add distractions and work in new environments. To add a minor self-correction for the down-stay, stand on the dog's leash after he lies down, allowing about three inches of slack. If tries to get up before you've said "OK," he'll discover it doesn't work.

Do not step on the leash to make your dog lie down! This could badly hurt his neck, and will destroy his trust in you. Remember, we are teaching our dogs to make the best choices, not inflicting our answers upon them!

Come

Rather than thinking of "come" as an action—"come to me"—think of it as a place—"the dog is sitting in front of me, facing me." Since your dog by now really likes sitting to earn your touch and other positive reinforcement, he's likely to sometimes sit directly in front of you, facing you, all on his own. When this happens, give it a specific name: "come."

Now follow the rest of the training steps you have learned to make him like doing it and reinforce the behavior by practicing it any chance you get. Anything your dog wants and likes could be earned as a result of his first offering the sit-in-front known as "come."

You can help guide him into the right location. Use your hands as "landing gear" and pat the insides of your legs at his nose level. Do this while backing up a bit, to help him maneuver to the straight-in-front, facing-you position. Don't say the

Pat the insides of your legs to show your dog exactly where you like him to sit when you say "come."

word "come" while he's maneuvering, because he hasn't! You are trying to make "come" the end result, not the work in progress.

You can also help your dog by marking his movement in the right direction: Use your positive sound or word to promise he is getting warm. When he finally sits facing you, enthusiastically say "come," mark again with your positive word, and release him with an enthusiastic "OK!" Make it so worth his while, with lots of play and praise, that he can't wait for you to ask him to come again!

Building a Better Recall

Practice, practice, practice. Now, practice some more. Teach your dog that all good things in life hinge upon him first sitting in front of you in a behavior named "come." When you think he really has got it, test him by asking him to "come" as you gradually add distractions and change locations. Expect setbacks as you make these changes and practice accordingly. Lower your expectations and make his task easier so he is able to get it right. Use those distractions as rewards, when they are appropriate. For example, let him check out the interesting leaf that blew by as a reward for first coming to you and ignoring it.

Add distance and call your dog to come while he is on his retractable leash. If he refuses and sits looking at you blankly, *do not* jerk, tug, "pop," or reel him in. Do nothing! It is his move; wait to see what behavior he offers. He'll either begin to approach (mark the behavior with an excited "good!"), sit and do nothing (just keep waiting), or he'll try to move in some direction other than toward you. If he tries to leave, use your correction marker—"eh!"— and bring him to a stop by letting him walk to the end of the leash, *not* by jerking him. Now walk to him in a neutral manner, and don't jerk or show any disapproval. Gently bring him back to the spot where he was when you called him, then back away and face him, still waiting and not reissuing your command. Let him keep examining his options until he finds the one that works—yours!

If you have practiced everything I've suggested so far and given your dog a chance to really learn what "come" means, he is well aware of what you want and is quite intelligently weighing all his options. The only way he'll know your way is the one that works is to be allowed to examine his other choices and discover that they *don't* work.

Sooner or later every dog tests his training. Don't be offended or angry when your dog tests you. No matter how positive you've made it, he won't always want to do everything you ask, every time. When he explores the "what happens if I don't" scenario, your training is being strengthened. He will discover through his own process of trial and error that the best—and only—way out of a command he really doesn't feel compelled to obey is to obey it.

Let's Go

Many pet owners wonder if they can retain control while walking their dogs and still allow at least some running in front, sniffing, and playing. You might worry that allowing your dog occasional freedom could result in him expecting it all the time, leading to a testy, leash-straining walk. It's possible for both parties on the leash to have an enjoyable experience by implementing and reinforcing well-thought-out training techniques.

Begin by making word associations you'll use on your walks. Give the dog some slack on the leash, and as he starts to walk away from you say "OK" and begin to follow him.

Do not let him drag you; set the pace even when he is being given a turn at being the leader. Whenever he starts to pull, just come to a standstill and refuse to move (or refuse to allow him to continue forward) until there is slack in the leash. Do this correction without saying anything at all. When he isn't pulling, you may decide to just stand still and let him sniff about within the range the slack leash allows, or you may even mosey along following him. After a few minutes of "recess," it is time to work. Say something like "that's it" or "time's up," close the distance between you and your dog, and touch him.

Next say "let's go" (or whatever command you want to use to mean "follow me as we walk"). Turn and walk off, and, if he follows, mark his

Give your dog slack on his leash as you walk and let him make the decision to walk with you.

When your dog catches up with you, make sure you let him know what a great dog he is!

Intersperse periods of attentive walking, where your dog is on a shorter leash, with periods on a slack leash, where he is allowed to look and sniff around.

behavior with "good!" Then stop, squat down, and let him catch you. Make him glad he did! Start again, and do a few transitions as he gets the hang of your follow-the-leader game, speeding up, slowing down, and trying to make it fun. When you stop, he gets to catch up and receive some deserved positive reinforcement. Don't forget that's the reason he is following you, so be sure to make it worth his while!

Require him to remain attentive to you. Do not allow sniffing, playing, eliminating, or pulling during your time as leader on a walk. If he seems to get distracted—which, by the way, is the main reason dogs walk poorly with their people—change direction or pace without saying a word. Just help him realize "oops, I lost track of my human." Do not jerk his neck and say "heel"—this will make the word "heel" mean pain in the neck and will not encourage him to cooperate with you. Don't repeat "let's go," either. He needs to figure out that it is his job to keep track of and follow you if he wants to earn the positive benefits you provide.

The best reward you can give a dog for performing an attentive, controlled walk is a few minutes of walking without all of the controls. Of course, he must remain on a leash even during the "recess" parts of the walk, but allowing him to discriminate between attentive following—"let's go"—and having a few moments of relaxation—"OK"—will increase his willingness to work.

Training for Attention

Your dog pretty much has a one-track mind. Once he is focused on something, everything else is excluded. This can be great, for instance, when he's focusing on you! But it can also be dangerous if, for example, his attention is riveted on the bunny he is chasing and he does not hear you call—that is, not unless he has been trained to pay attention when you say his name.

When you say your dog's name, you'll want him to make eye contact with you. Begin teaching this by making yourself so intriguing that he can't help but look.

When you call your dog's name, you will again be seeking a specific response—eye contact. The best way to teach this is to trigger his alerting response by making a noise with your mouth, such as whistling or a kissing sound, and then immediately doing something he'll find very intriguing.

You can play a treasure hunt game to help teach him to regard his name as a request for attention. As a bonus, you can reinforce the rest of his new vocabulary at the same time.

Treasure Hunt

Make a kissing sound, then jump up and find a dog toy or dramatically raid the fridge and rather noisily eat a piece of cheese. After doing this twice, make a kissing sound and then look at your dog.

Of course he is looking at you! He is waiting to see if that sound—the kissing sound—means you're going to go hunting again. After all, you're so good at it! Because he is looking, say his name, mark with "good," then go hunting and find his toy. Release it to him with an "OK." At any point if he follows you, attach your "let's go!" command; if he leaves you, give permission with "OK."

Using this approach, he cannot be wrong—any behavior your dog offers can be named. You can add things like "take it" when he picks up a toy, and "thank you" when he happens to drop one. Many opportunities to make your new vocabulary meaningful and positive can be found within this simple training game.

Problems to watch out for when teaching the treasure hunt:

- You really do not want your dog to come to you when you call his name (later, when you try to engage his attention to ask him to stay, he'll already be on his way toward you). You just want him to look at you.
- Saying "watch me, watch me" doesn't teach your dog to *offer* his attention. It just makes you a background noise.
- Don't lure your dog's attention with the reward. Get his attention and then reward him for looking. Try holding a toy in one hand with your arm stretched out to your side. Wait until he looks at you rather than the toy. Now say his name then mark with "good!" and release the toy. As he goes for it, say "OK."

To get your dog's attention, try holding his toy with your arm out to your side. Wait until he looks at you, then mark the moment and give him the toy.

Teaching Cooperation

Never punish your dog for failing to obey you or try to punish him into compliance. Bribing, repeating yourself, and doing a behavior for him all avoid the real issue of dog training—his will. He must be helped to be willing, not made to achieve tasks. Good dog training helps your dog want to obey. He learns that he can gain what he values most through cooperation and compliance, and can't gain those things any other way.

Your dog is learning to *earn,* rather than expect, the good things in life. And you've become much more important to him than you were before. Because you are allowing him to experiment and learn, he doesn't have to be forced, manipulated, or bribed. When he wants something, he can gain it by cooperating with you. One of those "somethings"—and a great reward you shouldn't underestimate—is your positive attention, paid to him with love and sincere approval!

Chapter 10

Housetraining Your Yorkie

Excerpted from Housetraining: An Owner's Guide to a Happy Healthy Pet, 1st Edition, *by September Morn*

By the time puppies are about 3 weeks old, they start to follow their mother around. When they are a few steps away from their clean sleeping area, the mama dog stops. The pups try to nurse but mom won't allow it. The pups mill around in frustration, then nature calls and they all urinate and defecate here, away from their bed. The mother dog returns to the nest, with her brood waddling behind her. Their first housetraining lesson has been a success.

The next one to housetrain puppies should be their breeder. The breeder watches as the puppies eliminate, then deftly removes the soiled papers and replaces them with clean papers before the pups can traipse back through their messes. He has wisely arranged the puppies' space so their bed, food, and drinking water are as far away from the elimination area as possible. This way, when the pups follow their mama, they will move away from their sleeping and eating area before eliminating. This habit will help the pups be easily housetrained.

Your Housetraining Shopping List

While your puppy's mother and breeder are getting her started on good housetraining habits, you'll need to do some shopping. If you have all the essentials in place before your dog arrives, it will be easier to help her learn the rules from day one.

Newspaper: The younger your puppy and larger her breed, the more newspapers you'll need. Newspaper is absorbent, abundant, cheap, and convenient.

Puddle Pads: If you prefer not to stockpile newspaper, a commercial alternative is puddle pads. These thick paper pads can be purchased under several trade names at pet supply stores. The pads have waterproof backing, so puppy urine doesn't seep through onto the floor. Their disadvantages are that they will cost you more than newspapers and that they contain plastics that are not biodegradable.

Poop Removal Tool: There are several types of poop removal tools available. Some are designed with a separate pan and rake, and others have the handles hinged like scissors. Some scoops need two hands for operation, while others are designed for one-handed use. Try out the different brands at your pet supply store. Put a handful of pebbles or dog kibble on the floor and then pick them up with each type of scoop to determine which works best for you.

Plastic Bags: When you take your dog outside your yard, you *must* pick up after her. Dog waste is unsightly, smelly, and can harbor disease. In many cities and towns, the law mandates dog owners clean up pet waste deposited on public ground. Picking up after your dog using a plastic bag scoop is simple. Just put your hand inside the bag, like a mitten, and then grab the droppings. Turn the bag inside out, tie the top, and that's that.

Crate: To housetrain a puppy, you will need some way to confine her when you're unable to supervise. A dog crate is a secure way to confine your dog for short periods during the day and to use as a comfortable bed at night. Crates come in wire mesh and in plastic. The wire ones are foldable to store flat in a smaller space. The plastic ones are more cozy, draft-free, and quiet, and are approved for airline travel.

Baby Gates: Since you shouldn't crate a dog for more than an hour or two at a time during the day, baby gates are a good way to limit your dog's freedom in the house. Be sure the baby gates you use are safe. The old-fashioned wooden, expanding lattice type has seriously injured a number of children by collapsing and trapping a leg, arm, or neck. That type of gate can hurt a puppy, too, so use the modern grid type gates instead. You'll need more than one baby gate if you have several doorways to close off.

Exercise Pen: Portable exercise pens are great when you have a young pup or a small dog. These metal or plastic pens are made of rectangular panels that are hinged together. The pens are freestanding, sturdy, foldable, and can be carried like a suitcase. You could set one up in your kitchen as the pup's daytime corral, and then take it outdoors to contain your pup while you garden or just sit and enjoy the day.

Enzymatic Cleaner: All dogs make housetraining mistakes. Accept this and be ready for it by buying an enzymatic cleaner made especially for pet accidents. Dogs like to eliminate where they have done it before, and lingering smells lead them to those spots. Ordinary household cleaners may remove all the odors you can smell, but only an enzymatic cleaner will remove everything your dog can smell.

The First Day

Housetraining is a matter of establishing good habits in your dog. That means you never want her to learn anything she will eventually have to unlearn. Start off housetraining on the right foot by teaching your dog that you prefer her to eliminate outside. Designate a potty area in your backyard (if you have one) or in the street in front of your home and take your dog to it as soon as you arrive home. Let her sniff a bit and, when she squats to go, give the action a name: "potty" or "do it" or anything else you won't be embarrassed to say in public. Eventually your dog will associate that word with the act and will eliminate on command. When she's finished, praise her with "good potty!"

That first day, take your puppy out to the potty area frequently. Although she may not eliminate every time, you are establishing a routine: You take her to her

Don't Overuse the Crate

A crate serves well as a dog's overnight bed, but you should not leave the dog in her crate for more than an hour or two during the day. Throughout the day, she needs to play and exercise. She is likely to want to drink some water and will undoubtedly eliminate. Confining your dog all day will give her no option but to soil her crate. This is not just unpleasant for you and the dog, but it reinforces bad cleanliness habits. And crating a pup for the whole day is abusive. Don't do it.

spot, ask her to eliminate, and praise her when she does.

Just before bedtime, take your dog to her potty area once more. Stand by and wait until she produces. Do not put your dog to bed for the night until she has eliminated. Be patient and calm. This is not the time to play with or excite your dog. If she's too excited, a pup not only won't eliminate, she probably won't want to sleep either.

Most dogs, even young ones, will not soil their beds if they can avoid it. For this reason, a sleeping crate can be a tremendous help during housetraining. Being crated at night

Start off as you mean to continue; take your pup outside to eliminate right from day one.

can help a dog develop the muscles that control elimination. So after your dog has emptied out, put her to bed in her crate.

A good place to put your dog's sleeping crate is near your own bed. Dogs are pack animals, so they feel safer sleeping with others in a common area. In your bedroom, the pup will be near you and you'll be close enough to hear when she wakes during the night and needs to eliminate.

Pups under 4 months old often are not able to hold their urine all night. If your puppy has settled down to sleep but awakens and fusses a few hours later, she probably needs to go out. For the best housetraining progress, take your pup to her elimination area whenever she needs to go, even in the wee hours of the morning.

Your pup may soil in her crate if you ignore her late night urgency. It's unfair to let this happen, and it sends the wrong message about your expectations for cleanliness. Resign yourself to this midnight outing and just get up and take the pup out. Your pup will outgrow this need soon and will learn in the process that she can count on you, and you'll wake happily each morning to a clean dog.

The next morning, the very first order of business is to take your pup out to eliminate. Don't forget to take her to her special potty spot, ask her to eliminate, and then praise her when she does. After your pup empties out in the morning, give her breakfast, and then take her to her potty area again. After that, she shouldn't need to eliminate again right away, so you can allow her some free playtime. Keep an eye on the pup though, because when she pauses in play she may need to go potty. Take her to the right spot, give the command, and praise if she produces.

Confine Your Pup

A pup or dog who has not finished housetraining should *never* be allowed the run of the house unattended. A new dog (especially a puppy) with unlimited access to your house will make her own choices about where to eliminate. Vigilance during your new dog's first few weeks in your home will pay big dividends. Every potty mistake delays housetraining progress; every success speeds it along.

Prevent problems by setting up a controlled environment for your new pet. A good place for a puppy corral is often the kitchen. Kitchens almost always have waterproof or easily cleaned floors, which is a distinct asset with leaky pups. A bathroom, laundry room, or enclosed porch could be used for a puppy corral, but the kitchen is generally the best location. Kitchens are a meeting place and a hub of activity for many families, and a puppy will learn better manners when she is socialized thoroughly with family, friends, and nice strangers.

Confinement is one of the most important aspects of housetraining. Unlimited access to the house means unlimited choices about where to eliminate.

The way you structure your pup's corral area is very important. Her bed, food, and water should be at the opposite end of the corral from the potty area. When you first get your pup, spread newspaper over the rest of the floor of her playpen corral. Lay the papers at least four pages thick and be sure to overlap the edges. As you note the pup's progress, you can remove the papers nearest the sleeping and eating corner. Gradually decrease the size of the papered area until only the end where you want the pup to eliminate is covered. If you will be training your dog to eliminate outside, place newspaper at the end of the corral that is closest to the door that leads outdoors. That way as she moves away from the clean area to the papered area, the pup will also form the habit of heading toward the door to go out.

Maintain a scent marker for the pup's potty area by reserving a small soiled piece of paper when you clean up. Place this piece, with her scent of urine, under the top sheet of the clean papers you spread. This will cue your pup where to eliminate.

Most dog owners use a combination of indoor papers and outdoor elimination areas. When the pup is left by herself in the corral, she can potty on the ever-present newspaper. When you are available to take the pup outside, she can do her business in the outdoor spot. It is not difficult to switch a pup from indoor paper training to outdoor elimination. Owners of large pups often switch early, but potty papers are still useful if the pup spends time in her indoor corral while you're away. Use the papers as long as your pup needs them. If you come home and they haven't been soiled, you are ahead.

When setting up your pup's outdoor yard, put the lounging area as far away as possible from the potty area, just as with the indoor corral setup. People with large yards, for example, might leave a patch unmowed at the edge of the lawn to serve as the dog's elimination area.

> **TIP**
>
> **Water**
>
> Make sure your dog has access to clean water at all times. Limiting the amount of water a dog drinks is not necessary for housetraining success and can be very dangerous. A dog needs water to digest food, to maintain a proper body temperature and proper blood volume, and to clean her system of toxins and wastes. A healthy dog will automatically drink the right amount. Do not restrict water intake. Controlling your dog's access to water is not the key to housetraining her; controlling her access to everything else in your home is.

Other dog owners teach the dog to relieve herself in a designated corner of a deck or patio. For an apartment-dwelling city dog, the outdoor potty area might be a tiny balcony or the curb. Each dog owner has somewhat different expectations for their dog. Teach your dog to eliminate in a spot that suits your environment and lifestyle.

Be sure to pick up droppings in your yard at least once a day. Dogs have a natural desire to stay far away from their own excrement, and if too many piles litter the ground, your dog won't want to walk through it and will start eliminating elsewhere. Leave just one small piece of feces in the potty area to remind your dog where the right spot is located.

To help a pup adapt to the change from indoors to outdoors, take one of her potty papers outside to the new elimination area. Let the pup stand on the paper when she goes potty outdoors. Each day for four days, reduce the size of the paper by half. By the fifth day, the pup, having used a smaller and smaller piece of paper to stand on, will probably just go to that spot and eliminate.

City dogs will need to learn to eliminate out in the street. It's no problem for your smart Yorkie!

Backyard potty breaks should be all business. Don't let your pup turn them into playtime.

Take your pup to her outdoor potty place frequently throughout the day. A puppy can hold her urine for only about as many hours as her age in months, and will move her bowels as many times a day as she eats. So a 2-month-old pup will urinate about every two hours, while at 4 months she can manage about four hours between piddles. Pups vary somewhat in their rate of development, so this is not a hard and fast rule. It does, however, present a realistic idea of how long a pup can be left without access to a potty place. Past 4 months, her potty trips will be less frequent.

When you take the dog outdoors to her spot, keep her leashed so that she won't wander away. Stand quietly and let her sniff around in the designated area. If your pup starts to leave before she has eliminated, gently lead her back and remind her to go. If your pup sniffs at the spot, praise her calmly, say the command word, and just wait. If she produces, praise serenely, then give her time to sniff around a little more. She may not be finished, so give her time to go again before allowing her to play and explore her new home.

If you find yourself waiting more than five minutes for your dog to potty, take her back inside. Watch your pup carefully for twenty minutes, not giving her any opportunity to slip away to eliminate unnoticed. If you are too busy to watch the pup, put her in her crate.

After twenty minutes, take her to the outdoor potty spot again and tell her what to do. If you're unsuccessful after five minutes, crate the dog again. Give her another chance to eliminate in fifteen or twenty minutes. Eventually, she will have to go.

Watch Your Pup

Be vigilant and don't let the pup make a mistake in the house. Each time you successfully anticipate elimination and take your pup to the potty spot, you'll move a step closer to your goal. Stay aware of your puppy's needs. If you ignore the pup, she will make mistakes and you'll be cleaning up more messes.

Keep a chart of your new dog's elimination behavior for the first three or four days. Jot down what times she eats, sleeps, and eliminates. After several days a pattern will emerge that can help you determine your pup's body rhythms. Most dogs tend to eliminate at fairly regular intervals. Once you know your new dog's natural rhythms, you'll be able to anticipate her needs and schedule appropriate potty outings.

Understanding the meanings of your dog's postures can also help you win the battle of the puddle. When your dog is getting ready to eliminate, she will display a specific set of postures. The sooner you can learn to read these signals, the cleaner your floor will stay.

Eventually you will learn to read your dog's body language, and she will tell you when she needs to go out.

A young puppy who feels the urge to eliminate may start to sniff the ground and walk in a circle. If the pup is very young, she may simply squat and go. All young puppies, male or female, squat to urinate. If you are housetraining a pup under 4 months of age, regardless of sex, watch for the beginnings of a squat as the signal to rush the pup to the potty area.

When a puppy is getting ready to defecate, she may run urgently back and forth or turn in a circle while sniffing or starting to squat. If defecation is imminent, the pup's anus may protrude or open slightly. When she starts to go, the pup will squat and hunch her back, her tail sticking straight out behind. There is no mistaking this posture; nothing else looks like this. If your pup takes this position, take her to her potty area. Hurry! You may have to carry her to get there in time.

A young puppy won't have much time between feeling the urge and actually eliminating, so you'll have to be quick to note her postural clues and intercept your pup in time. Pups from 3 to 6 months have a few seconds more between the urge and the act than younger ones do. The older your pup, the more time you'll have to get her to the potty area after she begins the posture signals that alert you to her need.

Accidents Happen

If you see your pup about to eliminate somewhere other than the designated area, interrupt her immediately. Say "wait, wait, wait!" or clap your hands loudly to startle her into stopping. Carry the pup, if she's still small enough, or take her collar and lead her to the correct area. Once your dog is in the potty area, give her the command to eliminate. Use a friendly voice for the command, then wait patiently for her to produce. The pup may be tense because you've just startled her and may have to relax a bit before she's able to eliminate. When she does her job, include the command word in the praise you give ("good potty").

The old-fashioned way of housetraining involved punishing a dog's mistakes even before she knew what she was supposed to do. Puppies were punished for breaking rules they didn't understand about functions they couldn't control. This was not fair. While your dog is new to housetraining, there is no need or excuse for punishing her mistakes. Your job is to take the dog to the potty area just before she needs to go, especially with pups under 3 months old. If you aren't watching your pup closely enough and she has an accident, don't punish the puppy for your failure to anticipate her needs. It's not the pup's fault; it's yours.

In any case, punishment is not an effective tool for housetraining most dogs. Many will react to punishment by hiding puddles and feces where you won't find them right away (like behind the couch or under the desk). This eventually may lead to punishment after the fact, which leads to more hiding, and so on.

Instead of punishing for mistakes, stay a step ahead of potty accidents by learning to anticipate your pup's needs. Accompany your dog to the designated potty area when she needs to go. Tell her what you want her to do and praise her when she goes. This will work wonders. Punishment won't be necessary if you are a good teacher.

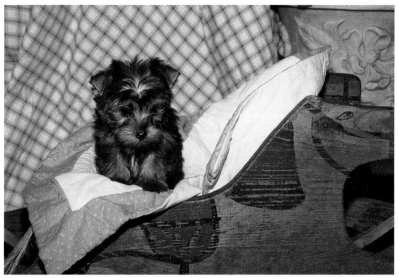

Instead of punishing your puppy for mistakes, set her up for success by getting her outside on a regular schedule.

What happens if you come upon a mess after the fact? Some trainers say a dog can't remember having eliminated, even a few moments after she has done so. This is not true. The fact is that urine and feces carry a dog's unique scent, which she (and every other dog) can instantly recognize. So, if you happen upon a potty mistake after the fact you can still use it to teach your dog.

But remember, no punishment! Spanking, hitting, shaking, or scaring a puppy for having a housetraining accident is confusing and counterproductive. Spend your energy instead on positive forms of teaching.

Take your pup and a paper towel to the mess. Point to the urine or feces and calmly tell your puppy, "no potty here." Then scoop or sop up the accident with the paper towel. Take the evidence and the pup to the approved potty area. Drop the mess on the ground and tell the dog, "good potty here," as if she had done the deed in the right place. If your pup sniffs at the evidence, praise her calmly. If the accident happened very recently your dog may not have to go yet, but wait with her a few minutes anyway. If she eliminates, praise her. Afterwards, go finish cleaning up the mess.

Soon the puppy will understand that there is a place where you are pleased about elimination and other places where you are not. Praising for elimination in the approved place will help your pup remember the rules.

Scheduling Basics

With a new puppy in the home, don't be surprised if your rising time is suddenly a little earlier than you've been accustomed to. Puppies have earned a reputation as very early risers. When your pup wakes you at the crack of dawn, you will have to get up and take her to her elimination spot. Be patient. When your dog is an adult, she may enjoy sleeping in as much as you do.

At the end of this chapter, you'll find a typical housetraining schedule for puppies aged 10 weeks to 6 months. (To find schedules for younger and older pups, and for adult dogs, visit this book's companion web site.) It's fine to adjust the rising times when using this schedule, but you should not adjust the intervals between feedings and potty outings unless your pup's behavior justifies a change. Your puppy can only meet your expectations in housetraining if you help her learn the rules.

Arrange your pup's schedule around her meal times. She'll need to eliminate soon after she eats.

Puppies need a potty break soon after they wake up from a nap.

The schedule for puppies is devised with the assumption that someone will be home most of the time with the pup. That would be the best scenario, of course, but it is not always possible.

You may be able to ease the problems of a latchkey pup by having a neighbor or friend look in on the pup at noon and take her to eliminate. A better solution might be hiring a pet sitter to drop by midday. A professional pet sitter will be knowledgeable about companion animals and can give your pup high-quality care and socialization. Some can even help train your pup in both potty manners and basic obedience. Ask your veterinarian and your dog-owning friends to recommend a good pet sitter.

If you must leave your pup alone during her early housetraining period, be sure to cover the entire floor of her corral with thick layers of overlapping newspaper. If you come home to messes in the puppy corral, just clean them up. Be patient—she's still a baby.

Use this schedule (and the ones on the companion web site) as a basic plan to help prevent housetraining accidents. Meanwhile, use your own powers of observation to discover how to best modify the basic schedule to fit your dog's unique needs. Each dog is an individual and will have her own rhythms, and each dog is reliable at a different age.

Schedule for Pups 10 Weeks to 6 Months

7:00 a.m.	Get up and take the puppy from her sleeping crate to her potty spot.
7:15	Clean up last night's messes, if any.
7:30	Food and fresh water.
7:45	Pick up the food bowl. Take the pup to her potty spot; wait and praise.
8:00	The pup plays around your feet while you have your breakfast.
9:00	Potty break (younger pups may not be able to wait this long).
9:15	Play and obedience practice.
10:00	Potty break.
10:15	The puppy is in her corral with safe toys to chew and play with.
11:30	Potty break (younger pups may not be able to wait this long).
11:45	Food and fresh water.
12:00 p.m.	Pick up the food bowl and take the pup to her potty spot.
12:15	The puppy is in her corral with safe toys to chew and play with.
1:00	Potty break (younger pups may not be able to wait this long).
1:15	Put the pup on a leash and take her around the house with you.
3:30	Potty break (younger pups may not be able to wait this long).
3:45	Put the pup in her corral with safe toys and chews for solitary play and/or a nap.
4:45	Potty break.
5:00	Food and fresh water.
5:15	Potty break.
5:30	The pup may play nearby (either leashed or in her corral) while you prepare your evening meal.

7:00	Potty break.
7:15	Leashed or closely watched, the pup may play and socialize with family and visitors.
9:15	Potty break (younger pups may not be able to wait this long).
10:45	Last chance to potty.
11:00	Put the pup to bed in her crate for the night.

Appendix

Learning More About Your Yorkie

Some Good Books

Arden, Darlene, *The Irrepressible Toy Dog*, Howell Book House, 1998.

Dunbar, Ian, *Before & After Getting Your Puppy: The Positive Approach to Raising a Happy, Healthy & Well-Behaved Dog*, New World Library, 2004.

Gordon, Joan B., *The New Complete Yorkshire Terrier*, Howell Book House, 1993.

Griffen, James M., and Liisa D. Carlson, *Dog Owner's Home Veterinary Handbook*, 3rd edition, Howell Book House, 2000.

Hart, Benjamin L, and Linette A. Hart, *The Perfect Puppy: How to Choose Your Dog by Its Behavior*, W.H. Freeman and Company, 1988.

Wood, Deborah, *Little Dogs: Training Your Pint-Sized Companion*, T.F.H. Publications, 2004.

Wynne, William A., *Yorkie Doodle Dandy: A Memoir*, Wynnesome Press, 1996.

Magazines and Newsletters

***Popular Dog Series*, Volume 16, 2nd Edition: Yorkshire Terriers**
Fancy Publications
P. O. Box 6050
Mission Vejo, CA 92690
(800) 738-2665
www.dogfancy.com

The Whole Dog Journal
Belvoir Publications
P.O. Box 2626
Greenwich, CT 06836
(800) 829-9165
www.whole-dog-journal.com

Health and Safety Resources

First-Aid Videotape

Pet Emergency First Aid: Dogs
Apogee Entertainment
159 Alpine Way
Boulder, CO 80304
(800) 210-5700

Poisoning Hotline

ASPCA Animal Poison Control Center (APCC)
1717 South Philo Road, Suite 36
Urbana, IL 61802
(888) 426-4435
www.apcc.aspca.org

Lost-Dog Registration Services

AKC Companion Animal Recovery
(800) 252-7894
www.akccar.org

PETtrac
(800) 336-2843
www.avidid.com

24PetWatch
(866) 597-2424
www.24petwatch.com

Petlink.net
(877) PET-LINK
www.petlink.net

Veterinary Associations

Academy of Veterinary Homeopathy (AVH)
P. O. Box 9280
Wilmington, DE 19809
(866) 652-1590
www.theavh.org

American Academy of Veterinary Acupuncture (AAVA)
66 Morris Avenue, Suite 2A
Springfield, NJ 7081
(973) 379-1100
www.aava.org

American Animal Hospital Association (AAHA)
P. O. Box 150899
Denver, CO 80215-0899
(303) 986-2800
www.aahanet.org

American Holistic Veterinary Medical Association (AHVMA)
2218 Old Emmorton Road
Bel Air, MD 21015
(410) 569-0795
www.ahvma.org

Out-and-About Resources

Dog Clubs

American Kennel Club (AKC)
260 Madison Avenue, 4th Floor
New York, NY 10016
(212) 696-8200
www.akc.org

The Yorkshire Terrier Club of America
LaDonna Reno, Secretary
3738 E. Highway 47
Winfield, MO 63387
ytca_sec@ytca.org
www.ytca.org

The Yorkshire Terrier Club of America Foundation (YTCA)
Sharon McCadam, Secretary
2901 E. Section Street
Mount Vernon, WA 98274

Yorkshire Terrier National Rescue (YTNR)
Mary Elizabeth Dugmore, President
(615) 746-4401
dugmore@bellsouth.net
www.yorkshireterrierrescue.com

Trainers

Association of Pet Dog Trainers (APDT)
5096 Sand Road SE
Iowa City, IA 52240
(800) PET-DOGS
information@apdt.com
www.apdt.com

The International Association of Animal Behavior Consultants (IAABC)
www.iaabc.org

Resources on the Web

The following Web sites offer a variety of experiences for the dog-loving Internet surfer. Some sites present specific breed information, while others provide quizzes and questionnaires to help you decide which dog breed is the best one for you and your family. You can view photographs, research breeders and rescue organizations in your area, find out the best ways to exercise or travel with your pet, or just discover more about *Canis familiaris*. Enjoy!

AKC Online Breeder Classifieds

www.akc.org/classified

This new service from the AKC puts potential puppy buyers in contact with breeders in their state who have puppies to sell. Breeders who are listed are not endorsed by the AKC, but they are members in good standing and their litters are registered.

Choosing the Perfect Dog

www.choosingtheperfectdog.net

Another good, all-purpose site for dog owners or dog-owner wannabes. Information is presented in a very organized manner, with helpful sidebars and links. Practical answers are given to questions such as "How do I match a dog to my lifestyle?" or "How much time/money/stuff do I need to provide for a dog?" The site prompts visitors to think carefully about getting a dog and to responsibly research dog breeds so that everyone involved lives happily ever after.

Dog Advisors

www.dogadvisors.com

This is a fun site where the fancier can delve a little deeper and learn a little more about his or her favorite dog breed. Different breeds are highlighted at various times, as are specific breeders.

Dog Breed Information Center

www.dogbreedinfo.com

This is a well-designed site with cute doggie graphics and easy-to-use links. Log on to donate toys to rescue organizations, post messages for like-minded dog folk, take questionnaires to discover which dog breed is best suited to your family and your home, view a plethora of canine photographs, or discover the answers to frequently asked dog-care and training questions.

Good News for Pets

www.goodnewsforpets.com

This weekly digest provides interesting tidbits on all things canine related. It profiles people who are active in the dog community, provides nutrition facts, addresses legal issues, and focuses attention on how dogs are portrayed in books and on film. Visit every Monday for the Pet Question of the Week.

Pets Welcome

www.petswelcome.com

If you plan on traveling with your pet, a visit to this site is a must. The listings page offers information on more than 25,000 hotels, bed & breakfasts, ski resorts, campgrounds, and pet-friendly beaches. Plenty of advice and knowledge are provided for those who can't imagine leaving their pet at home.

Vet Info.com

www.vetinfo.com

If your dog is suffering from a particular ailment, you can find out more about it by visiting vetinfo.com. The format of this site is easy to use, with each disease listed in alphabetical order. To delve even deeper into your pet's health, you might subscribe to *Vetinfo Digest* for its Ask Dr. Mike segment.

Index

commands
- come, 113–114
- down, 111–112
- let's go, 115–116
- OK, 111
- recall, 114
- sit, 110–111
- stay, 112–113

communications, training element, 109
companionship, characteristic, 22–24
consideration, senior dog care, 97
constipation, problem indicator, 84
cooperation, training techniques, 119
coughing, health problem, 84
CPR, techniques, 93
crates, 44–48, 121–123

diarrhea, health problem indicator, 84
diets
- age/lifestyle considerations, 53–54
- homemade foods, 56
- snacks/treats, 57–58

distemper, three-year vaccine, 73
dog shows, breeder resource, 36
down command, training, 111–112
dry foods, pros/cons, 53

ears
- breed standard element, 15
- health indicator, 81
- senior dog issues, 94–95
- sound sensitivity, 26

elimination habits, health indicator, 79
England, history, 20–22
enzymatic cleaners, housetraining, 122
exercise pens, housetraining, 121–122
expression, breed characteristic, 15
eye rubbing, problem indicator, 87
eyes
- breed standard element, 15
- health indicator, 81
- nearsightedness, 26
- senior dog issues, 94–95

females, spay benefits, 76–77
first-aid kit, components, 92
fleas, prevention methods, 65–69
focus (attention), training, 116–119
foods
- AAFCO (American Association of Feed Control Officials), 54
- age considerations, 53–54
- dry versus canned, 53
- feeding do's/don'ts, 58
- feeding timelines, 56–57
- label information, 54
- life stage considerations, 53–54
- natural ingredients, 55
- organically grown, 55
- pet versus people, 56
- snacks, 57–58
- treats, 57–58

food/water dishes, purchasing, 44
found (stray) dogs, 34–35
FrontLine Plus, flea prevention, 67

genitals, health indicator, 82–83
giardia, internal parasite, 91
grooming
- anal sacs, 82
- baths, 64–65
- brushing/combing, 61–62
- chews/toy avoidance, 61
- coat parting, 70
- ears, 81
- eyes, 81
- nail trimming, 65
- routines, 60, 63
- senior dogs, 96
- teeth, 81
- tools, 45, 49, 60
- topknots, 70
- trimming techniques, 62–64

grooming table, 60

harness, purchasing guidelines, 45
heads, breed standard element, 13

Photo Credits:

Jeannie Harrison: title page, 14, 28, 33, 34, 40–41, 48, 49, 52, 53, 57, 59, 62, 63, 64, 65, 75, 79, 81, 86, 120, 123, 124, 126, 127, 130, 131
Kent Dannen: 8–9, 11, 13, 17, 18, 19, 23, 25, 27, 30, 31, 36, 37, 42, 43, 50, 55, 61, 66, 71, 74, 78, 80, 82, 83, 85, 87, 88, 90, 93, 96, 98–99, 129
Howell Book House: 10, 21, 22